*I am sending the enclosed book
as a gift to Tennessee libraries.
The book is a collection of the McWherter
early years and the events that took place
in Tennessee state government during the last part
of the Twentieth Century.
I will be forever grateful to the thousands
of Tennesseans who supported me over the years.*

Ned R. McWherter
Governor, State Of Tennessee
1987-1995

McWherter

The Life and Career of Ned McWherter

Billy Stair

To Savannah Stair, Lucille and Harmon McWherter

CONTENTS

FOREWARD

All of us see the world through our own eyes. In that sense, the following story is neither complete nor unbiased. This book is not a scholarly work; it is a collection of events and anecdotes that attempts to tell the story of someone who influenced not just the modern history of Tennessee, but also those of us whose lives he touched over much of his career. By choice, the story is told largely by Ned McWherter himself, and by the friends and staff who were closest to him. The descriptions of some events were drawn from memories that have faded over time. Other parts of the story came from those of us whose objectivity was no doubt affected by the intense emotions that accompany political campaigns and the legislative process. For that reason alone, both our opponents and our friends will certainly remember some of the story's events differently. To those whose names were omitted, or whose accomplishments were not done justice, the fault was not intentional.

One of the greatest challenges was deciding which parts of the story were most important. The limits of time and the passing of those involved made it necessary to leave out dozens of issues and events that are worthy of more detail. For the early part of his life, the story focuses on the people and events that shaped McWherter's core beliefs and his unique political talents. The selected anecdotes from his career as Speaker and Governor, and particularly from the two years of his gubernatorial campaign, are an effort to reveal who he was as much as what he did.

Perhaps most important, this story is for our children. Years from now, the McWherter Administration will likely be remembered as most others in Tennessee. History books will have a short paragraph and, perhaps, a picture of the Governor. Readers of these books would not know that those of us who served with Ned McWherter always thought of ourselves as part of an extended family. In the years after his retirement in 1995, we often came together for summer picnics or Christmas reunions. We celebrated each other's accomplishments and shared in the grief when death called our colleagues or their family members. The size of this extended McWherter family, and the love that they shared, are unlike any in memory. For the members of this family, it is important for our children to read this story, with the hope that they will share our pride in being part of a special moment in Tennessee history.

Billy Stair

PART ONE

THE EARLY YEARS

1930-1968

THE EARLY YEARS

1930-1968

We are all a product of time and place.

One of the most prominent Tennesseans of the 20th Century was born in a Sharecropper's house. Ned Ray McWherter came into the world near the small community of Palmersville on October 15, 1930. Located in Weakley County, Palmersville was typical of small towns in rural Northwest Tennessee where everybody knew everybody else and most families were related. Literally a wide place in the road, Palmersville consisted of a grocery store, a feed and grain mill, the obligatory filling station, a small school, and a few homes. The largest building in the community was, and still is, the Masonic Lodge, a two story clapboard structure erected in 1847.

By the time Ned was born, the McWherter family was already well established in Weakley County. The cemetery, next to the Masonic Lodge and established in 1872, contains eighteen gravestones designating various members of the McWherter family, the oldest belonging to H. C. McWherter, born in 1856.

McWherter's parents, Lucille Golden Smith McWherter and Harmon Ray McWherter, both grew up in the area. His mother, one of five children, was known by everyone as Miss Lucille. She was born in the Weakley County village, no longer there, with the quaint name of The Number One Community. She attended school in Weakley County through the eighth grade, when her formal education ended. Miss Lucille and her family were leading members of the Bethany Church of Christ, which has since burned, although the cemetery still exists. Miss Lucille was known for a kind disposition and quick wit. Those who knew both Miss Lucille and her son Ned said he inherited those characteristics.

Harmon McWherter came from a family of sharecroppers. After the third grade, he dropped out of school to help his two brothers, parents and grandparents work the land. Ned remembers an early picture of his mother and father, taken while they were courting. They were perched on the seat of a "good looking horse and buggy, so apparently somewhere along the way my dad had made a good potato crop and he had a little money." After Harmon and Miss Lucille married, they continued to make their living as tenant farmers, raising corn, potatoes and chickens.

Ned McWherter was born one year into the Great Depression, a period that was especially hard in rural West Tennessee. Harmon and Miss Lucille McWherter occupied a white, four-room frame house, with a tin roof and an outside toilet, located six miles from Palmersville in the Little Zion Community. The living room fireplace was the only source of heat in the winter. Miss Lucille cooked on a wood stove in the kitchen.

When McWherter turned three, his mother and father moved in with his grandfather Tobe McWherter, who also lived in the Little Zion community. A widower, Tobe was grateful for the help and the company. The Little Zion Baptist church, a "foot washin' Baptist" congregation, still stands. His grandfather is buried in the church cemetery.

McWherter entered the first grade in the one-room Little Zion School, where Miss Valda Stewart taught all eight grades. The children were grouped according to age, with three or four children in each "class." Each class had a designated spot in the room, with the younger children in the corners and the older ones clustered in the center. Total enrollment in the Little Zion School hovered between fifteen and twenty students, the numbers growing in the winter and slacking off in the spring and fall as the children helped in the fields. The Little Zion School was heated by a wood burning stove. The pupils would warm their lunches, often a single sweet potato, in the ashes. At recess the boys played basketball on a dirt court and the girls stood in small groups under the trees. His first teacher would prove to be a major influence in McWherter's life. He remembered Miss Stewart, a stickler for correct grammar, constantly admonishing her pupils to sit up straight at their desks. Reflecting on Miss Stewart, McWherter recalled, "She was an excellent teacher and set good examples for all of us in that little one room school. We got a good education and, most of all, we respected her."

Miss Stewart had no reservations about corporal punishment. In the fall, when the crops were ready for harvest, some of her more rambunctious students, McWherter included, would sneak out behind the schoolhouse during recess and twist into homemade cigarettes the silk from the feed corn. Smoking the corn silk would inevitably burn their mouths, making it possible to identify the guilty boys. "She'd whip us with a paddle," McWherter admitted, with a wry smile, "She needed to."

In the mid 1930s, Weakley County in general and Little Zion in particular were more rural than even most Tennessee communities. The majority of people traveled in horse drawn wagons and buggies. When the weather was fair, McWherter would walk to school. In the winter, the bottomland would be soaked from the rain and snow, and the roads, difficult in the best of weather, became impassable. On harsh winter mornings, Harmon McWherter would pull on his work boots, lift his son onto the back of their horse, and walk to the nearby farms where he would, one by one, collect the other school children. Harmon would load up the horse with four or five kids and lead them through the soggy or frozen bottomland to the school.

Although the Tennessee Valley Authority brought electricity to the region around 1935, power did not reach rural Weakley County until 1937. On cloudy days the school's only light came from coal oil lamps. McWherter did his homework by the glow of an Aladdin kerosene lamp.

In 1942, the McWherters moved into Palmersville proper, but did not yet own their own house. They shared the home of Miss Florence LaFon, a cousin of Miss Lucille's childhood friend Pauline Gore. The house in Palmersville had electricity, running water and a party telephone line, complete with a local switchboard operator. Each family was assigned a telephone code. The subscribers could tell by the pattern of the ring whose house was being called. Different rings did not stop residents from listening in to everyone else's conversations. Local news spread quickly, if not always accurately.

By 1942, America had entered the Second World War. Harmon McWherter, at thirty-seven, was too old for the draft. The automobile assembly plants in Michigan had been converted to the manufacturing of tanks and airplanes for the war, attracting many rural Tennesseans who migrated north in search of higher paying jobs. Harmon joined them, leaving Palmersville to take a place on the production line at the Willow Run bomber plant in Ypsilanti, Michigan. Miss Lucille and Ned joined him six months later. Lucille's brother managed a White Castle hamburger restaurant in nearby Ann Arbor. He arranged for Miss Lucille to get a job at the Ypsilanti White Castle as a cook, the first job she ever had that did not involve working in the fields. The McWherters rented a small apartment in Ypsilanti, living "up North" for nearly three years.

The years in Michigan left a lasting impression on McWherter. Coming from segregated rural West Tennessee, he had never attended school with black children. In Michigan, one of his fifth grade classmates was a black boy whose father was a dentist. Miss Lucille had suffered intermittent problems with her teeth but had never found a suitable dentist in Northwest Tennessee. At home dentists were willing to extract the offending teeth, but they were not skilled at filling cavities. When she was again bothered with a toothache in Ypsilanti, McWherter mentioned his mother to his classmate. The boy told his father, who suggested Miss Lucille stop by his office. Although she eventually had her teeth pulled, the Ypsilanti dentist immediately fitted her with dentures. Miss Lucille, always full of spunk, loved to tell the story that a black dentist fit her with her first—and best—set of false teeth. McWherter today speaks fondly of the dentist's son and his family, with whom he became fast friends. "They were more educated than we were and more affluent. They were a nice family, and very kind to us."

After the German surrender in May of 1945, the McWherters returned to Weakley County, this time to Dresden, the county seat, where Harmon was hired by the Weakley County Highway Department. Not long after the McWherter's return to Tennessee, the Proctor and Gamble Ammunition Plant in Milan, about fifty miles south of Dresden, was awarded a contract to produce ammunition for the war with Japan. Both Harmon and Miss Lucille were hired at the ammunition factory, but they worked in separate buildings and usually on different shifts. The plant offered transportation for its employees. Each day a bus would pick up the workers in Dresden and the other small towns in the area and deposit them at the factory in Milan. As shifts ended, the bus made the return route. As a seventh grader in Dresden, McWherter often would eat breakfast with one of his parents and dinner with the other.

Like many families, the McWherters had prospered financially during the war. They purchased for $4,100 a six room frame house on sixty-five acres just outside the Dresden city limits, on old Highway 22 toward Gleason. McWherter's parents had saved $2,000 for the down payment and borrowed the rest. The home was the nicest in which they had ever lived. However, when the Japanese surrendered in August 1945 and work inevitably slowed at the Milan ammunition factory, Harmon and Miss Lucille were laid off. They sold their house and the sixty-five acres to Curtis Perry, who converted the property into a slaughterhouse. The McWherters this time moved within the Dresden city limits into a white frame house on the corner of Cedar and Evergreen Streets. Harmon returned to the highway department. Miss Lucille took a position as a seamstress at a shirt factory and later at the Bay-Bee Shoes Company in Dresden.

During McWherter's sophomore year at Dresden High School, his parents exhibited the same sense of business risk that would later characterize their son. They quit their respective jobs and for $2,200 purchased the City Café, a small restaurant one-half block off Dresden's court square. A local businessman, Carlos Brundige, loaned them the money. Miss Lucille had learned the restaurant business at the White Castle during their time in Ypsilanti. In Dresden, she handled the cooking. Harmon, who preferred not to work in the kitchen and "despised doing the dishes," operated the cash register. He also enjoyed sitting at a back table where he could swap local news with the customers. The restaurant was a family business in every aspect. Ned lent a hand, after school, on weekends and during the weekday lunch hour as well. He would leave Dresden High School a few minutes before noon to assist with the regular lunchtime crowd, many of whom were employees of the Bay-Bee Shoes factory. The City Café became a mainstay establishment in downtown Dresden, with community groups meeting in a private area dubbed the Club Room. The Dresden Rotary met on Tuesdays and the local Lions Club, of which McWherter later was a charter member, held weekly meetings at the City Café every Monday. In the post-World War II years, plate lunches cost sixty-five cents and coffee was a nickel. McWherter took orders, bussed tables and washed dishes. He often grabbed leftover food and wolfed it down on his way back to school. In subtle ways he likely did not think about as he worked in the little restaurant, the teenage McWherter grew to understand the importance and the unique needs of Tennessee's small business community.

The restaurant also played a significant role in shaping McWherter's attitudes about race relations. In

1970, more than two decades after McWherter worked there as a boy, the City Café became the site of Dresden's desegregation. McWherter was a freshman member of the Tennessee General Assembly. A black legislative colleague from Memphis, Ira Murphy, was an attorney who had a case in Dresden involving a car accident. He called McWherter to ask about hotel accommodations in town. Murphy had been informed blacks could not stay in Dresden, and that he would probably have to book a room in Milan or Fulton, Kentucky. McWherter told Murphy that he would try to get him a room at the Byars Hotel in Dresden. Barring that, Murphy was told he could spend the night at McWherter's home. McWherter also invited Murphy to join him for lunch at the City Café.

Murphy and his associate, another black man, arrived in Dresden on a Friday morning after the legislative session in Nashville had adjourned for the week. When they broke for lunch, they crossed the street from the court house, walked down an alley and entered the back door of the City Café. Miss Lucille introduced herself to the gentlemen, who had ordered the plate lunch and were seated in the back of the restaurant at a little round table covered with oil cloth. Murphy and Miss Lucille chatted and in the course of the conversation, Miss Lucille suddenly said, "This has gone on long enough. If you can serve in the legislature with my son, you can eat with my son." She escorted the men out front and seated them in the middle of the restaurant. McWherter later remarked with pride that he never saw another black person sit at the back of the City Café. Three years later, when he was elected Speaker of the House, McWherter appointed Ira Murphy as Chair of the House Judiciary Committee, the first black committee chair in the South.

Harmon and Miss Lucille McWherter developed strong ties with other small business owners in Dresden during the years after World War II. Several other couples, all of whom ran a business on or near the court square, became close and lifelong friends. M. F. and Ruel Riggs, along with Edith and S.T. Bowlin, owned the Bowlin and Riggs Funeral Home. George and Peggy Mayo operated the Western Auto store located next door to the City Café. Ibbie and Luther Kelly had Kelly's Dry Goods Store. Raymond and Mattie Lee Bradberry owned a dry cleaners and a small restaurant called the Donut Shop. Located next to the Bowlin and Riggs Funeral Home, the Donut Shop's walls were covered with pictures of the Dresden basketball and football teams and emerged as a popular local hangout for young people. High school students dropped in after school to drink Coca-Cola and listen to rock and roll. Younger children showed up for ice cream and hot chocolate. Across from the Donut Shop was a small hill. When it snowed, the local children would sled down the hill until their clothes were soaking wet. They would stop by the dry cleaners and deposit their coats and mittens on the steam press to dry. Taking advantage of the opportunity, they would march next door to guzzle hot chocolate at The Donut Shop. McWherter's youth in many ways was Norman Rockwell's America.

Among those Dresden friends, only two couples had children. In addition to the McWherters, Raymond and Mattie Lee Bradberry were the parents of a daughter, Madelyn, born in 1944. Despite their age difference, Madelyn and Ned became friends. The friendship blossomed into a business relationship that lasted throughout their lives.

At her dad's Donut Shop, Madelyn peeled and sliced the onions, patted out the beef, and pulled the meat from the barbecued pork shoulders. Raymond made his own ice cream. He invented more than thirty flavors years before Baskin-Robbins. In the late 1940s, black children would come to town "out of the bottom" with just enough money for an ice cream cone. In a time when blacks could not enter restaurants, the children would stand at the doorway of the Donut Shop. Miss Willie, who by Madelyn's own admission "did everything" at the Donut Shop, would take their orders. Raymond always treated them to a free cone.

Dresden was located in the middle of St. Louis Cardinals baseball territory. Raymond Bradberry owned one of the area's few sound systems. He and Carmack Anderson would drive to the Dresden football field, temporarily remove some of the wooden bleachers, and assemble them on a small hill across from the Donut Shop, the same hill where the children rode their sleds. At night, Raymond would pipe the Cardinals games out through a transom over the door of the dry cleaners, set up a popcorn machine and a cooler of Coke, and invite the townspeople to listen to the St. Louis radio broadcast. Popcorn sold for a dime and Cokes for a nickel.

As a young man, McWherter was tall and powerfully built. As is often the case with successful men and women, he was a natural leader in high school. The Dresden public library, which McWherter built after he came back home from his time as Governor, has a room dedicated to him. The pictures on the walls reveal the kind of charisma and leadership ability that are difficult to define but easy to recognize. By the time he graduated from Dresden High School in 1948, McWherter had been class vice president, co-captain of the football team, a guard on the basketball team, and voted "best looking" by his fellow classmates. Always a natty dresser, McWherter's senior class picture shows him in a double-breasted linen suit and a bow tie. Also prominently displayed in the library is his blue corduroy Future Farmers of America jacket, enclosed in a clear plastic case. "President" is embroidered in gold thread high on the right breast.

McWherter credits his FFA advisor, Mr. V. J. Shanklin, with teaching him many of the skills and values that served him well throughout both his business and political careers. In particular, V. J. Shanklin made sure McWherter was well trained in the arcane skills of parliamentary procedure, an important aspect of every Future Farmers of America meeting. The early training in parliamentary procedure paid off two decades later when McWherter ran for Speaker of the Tennessee House. The legislature contained numerous skeptics who believed McWherter could never make an effective Speaker of the House because he could not master the complex rules the House used to conduct business. Privately, McWherter himself was not completely sure he would be able to preside as Speaker. Nevertheless, he boasted, "You just elect me, and I'll show you." McWherter's confidence was well-founded. "When I did get elected and I knew parliamentary procedure from my time as president of the Dresden High School Future Farmers of America Club, I realized the small things I had learned growing up in rural Northwest Tennessee related to the big things in Nashville. I did just fine."

McWherter's high school years were little different from those of his friends and classmates. One such experience they shared on occasion was drinking home brew. On a particularly memorable night, McWherter drove his father's 1936 Chevrolet into a ditch. This and similar incidents disappointed his mother.

While McWherter maintained a life-long devotion to his mother, even at an early age he displayed a streak of independence. Although Miss Lucille was a devout member of the Bethel Church of Christ, "a corner post," in McWherters words, he did not attend church with his mother. The decision caused a slight rift between them. In high school he started attending the Dresden Methodist Church, where he maintained his membership throughout his life.

Perhaps more significantly, McWherter also did not embrace his mother's career plans for him. Miss Lucille had her heart set on her son studying medicine and offered to do anything to help him become a doctor. Unfortunately for his mother, throughout high school McWherter only had two serious ambitions—to play football and to become a highway patrolman.

In addition to choices about church and career, McWherter was gradually developing other fundamental values and skills in his formative years. He listened to those with more experience and wisdom. He honed what became an extraordinary ability to communicate with various groups of people. Over time, he came to appreciate the connection between education and success.

V. J. Shanklin's wife taught English at Dresden High School and served as advisor to the Beta Club, a society for honor students. Although McWherter was capable of being a good student, academics were not always his priority in high school. When he applied himself and his grades were good, he would be asked to join the Beta Club. When his marks would drop, he would be expelled from the club. By his own admission, he "wore the door out getting in and out of the Beta Club." Mrs. Shanklin, whom McWherter describes as a wonderful lady and great teacher, became "a private tutor you never requested if you didn't make your grades."

The private tutoring did not end at graduation. In the years after he went to Nashville, Mrs. Shanklin critiqued his speeches whenever she saw them in print. A few days after a speech was publicized, one of Tennessee's most powerful individuals invariably received a succinct note from Mrs. Shanklin. The letter contained a copy of the speech with "good English" or "bad grammar" penned neatly in the margin. Throughout his public career, Mrs. Shanklin's comments were never far from his mind.

Although the 1948 graduating class at Dresden High School consisted of only seventeen students, the class contained several young men and women who would leave a mark on their community and their state. One of McWherter's classmates, Frank Rawls, earned a masters degree in transportation from the University of Tennessee and became vice president of transportation for the Eastman Kodak Corporation in Rochester, New York. Years later when the National Transportation Association held a conference at the Opryland Hotel in Nashville, Rawls was the keynote speaker. McWherter, by then Governor, was invited to welcome the group to Tennessee. McWherter warned Rawls ahead of time, "Now, Frank, when I introduce you and you make your remarks, we have to make an audio tape of our speeches and send the tapes to Mrs. Shanklin." McWherter advised Rawls not to make any mistakes because the governor himself planned to be "damn careful" not to make any. They made the tape and sent it to Ms. Shanklin who, even though she was ill, still considered both Rawls and McWherter her pupils. McWherter recalled Mrs. Shanklin fondly. "In a kind way, Mrs. Shanklin always intended for me to do well, from the time I was in her high school English class until the time she left this world."

Although McWherter was a leader in high school, the path to his high school diploma was neither a smooth nor an easy one. While playing football during his junior year, he hurt his knee, stopped going to practice, and eventually dropped out of school. Tom Reagan, "the best mechanic in Dresden," was co-owner of the local Pontiac dealership and was a football standout at Dresden some years before. During McWherter's years on the high school team, Reagan worked on the sidelines at the games.

One day shortly after McWherter quit school, Reagan noticed the boy walking home from work at the City Café. Reagan stepped out on the sidewalk in front of the Pontiac dealership, greasy and dirty, and called to the young McWherter. "Ned, I want to talk to you. I want you to go back to school."

Ned shuffled his feat and replied, "Mr. Tom, I think I'm going to go to work."

Reagan persisted. "Ned, let me tell you one thing. You see these coveralls? You see how dirty and greasy they are? This is the only way I can make a living, because I only have an eighth grade education. Look over there in that bank. You look out front here at the Pontiac dealership and see who is running the sales. Those people have good, clean jobs. I've got a hard, dirty, greasy job. There's a better living for you if you go back to school and get an education. I don't know if you'll ever be a football star, but if you don't go back to school, you'll end up in overalls like these." With a decision that shaped the rest of his life, McWherter returned to high school, rejoined the football team and, in this case, pleased his mother.

After graduation McWherter wasted no time getting a full-time job. His first job was at the Bay-Bee Shoe Company in downtown Dresden, the same factory his mother had left to open the City Café. Bay-Bee Shoe Company was owned by three members of the Drerup family, another well known Northwest Tennessee name. A. L. Drerup, Sr. was president, his son Jack was the sales manager, and another son, W. E. (Pinky), managed the production line. Another of McWherter's high school classmates was a young woman named Eileen Wilson, whom he dated occasionally and escorted when she reigned as Queen of the Humboldt Strawberry Festival. Eileen eventually married Pinky Drerup. She and Pinky set up housekeeping in Dresden. The three remained friends until Pinky's death in 2004.

As the name suggested, Bay-Bee manufactured children's shoes. In the early days of Bay-Bee's operations, McWherter helped assemble the machines in the plant and worked a machine called a "pullover." He was not involved in the manufacturing end of the operation very long before Jack Drerup promoted him to work in the office as shipping clerk and delivery assistant. Bay-Bee produced children's shoes for a number of national outlets, including Sears, Kinney's, Bakers and McClellans. Part of McWherter's new job was to deliver the shoes to these outlets throughout the South.

McWherter's time at Bay-Bee Shoes was another formative period. He pays tribute to A. L. Drerup for giving him the chance to learn the shoe business and, perhaps more important, showing him how to live. McWherter recalls those times. "A. L. Drerup was an amazing man. In his day, he was an extremely astute businessman. He became an excellent marketing man before the term was common. He knew how to purchase leather and set competitive prices. He was very even tempered and a good listener. If you asked him for advice, he was always willing to give it. If you listened to him, his advice was pretty much on target."

Over the years McWherter received a great deal of sound advice from Drerup. In 1949, a year after McWherter graduated from high school, Drerup encouraged him to go to college. McWherter insisted he needed to work in order to buy a car. Drerup instead arranged for McWherter to enroll at the University of Tennessee at Martin, where he tried out for the football team. He was plagued, however, by his high school knee injury. McWherter dropped out after two weeks and returned to the shoe factory. In the spring of 1950, McWherter went back to UT Martin for spring training, with the hope of obtaining a football scholarship. He again re-injured his knee and was forced to quit.

The following year McWherter and Jack Smith, a friend from nearby McKenzie, attended summer football practice at Memphis State University. They both tried out as tackles under coach Ralph Hadley. Once again McWherter hoped to attend college on a football scholarship, but again he injured his knee. He returned to Dresden and went back to work for the Bay-Bee Shoe Company.

Whether stubborn or determined, in 1951 McWherter tried out for the Murray State University football team in Murray, Kentucky. When he damaged his knee for the fourth time, he finally abandoned his dream of attending college and playing football. His attention turned to building a career.

Yet another experience in his early years had a lasting impact on McWherter's philosophy. He joined the Tennessee National Guard while still in high school. His parents signed the paperwork even though he was legally too young to enlist. He joined the National Guard unit in Dresden. He was sworn in as a private in the twelve-member A Company by Judge Charles Butts in a tiny office beneath the Byars Hotel on the Dresden Court Square. The National Guard paid thirty dollars a month, an amount McWherter admitted "was good money back then." Butts, a Dresden native who organized A Company after World War II, served as the unit's commander. McWherter attended high school with Butt's younger brother James, called "Dukesy" by his friends. The two young men joined the National Guard together. Lacking any proper training ground, A Company conducted drills on the street in front of the Weakley County Court House. McWherter approached the National Guard with the same dedication and energy he applied to his job. From the day in 1948 when he first enlisted until he retired as a major in 1969, McWherter never missed a summer National Guard Camp. Even as House Speaker, he regularly visited with Tennessee Guard units at summer camp in Georgia and Mississippi. Years later when he ran for public office, his statewide support from Guard members played an important role in his success.

By 1951, more than a year into the Korean War, McWherter had attained the rank of staff sergeant. Thinking he could be ordered to Korea at any time, he attended NCO training and was promoted to tech sergeant. Although he was never sent to Korea, McWherter was active in the National Guard throughout the war. He received further training in Fort Benning, Georgia, at the Sandhill Ranger Camp. He recalled his stint in Fort Benning, as the "ninety-day wonder camp." To his buddies McWherter had always claimed he would do anything in the National Guard, "except crawl under live fire with machine guns shooting over me." As part of the Ranger training, the guardsmen found themselves in a trench with live ammunition overhead. "We couldn't get out of it, so I just did it."

Training with live ammunition was not his most challenging assignment. While at Fort Benning, McWherter made his one—and only—parachute jump. Like many young men, McWherter at the time thought he was a hot shot. Although he could not play college football, he believed he could do virtually everything else. Part of the Rangers training included learning to become efficient load masters by balancing the cargo in a DC-3. McWherter's squad was ordered to load a DC-3, throw the cargo out, then parachute from the airborne plane. Lingering toward the end of the line,

McWherter watched nervously as each of the other Rangers ejected their load and parachuted from the plane. When his turn came to execute the drill, he did as ordered, pushing out the cargo and opening his chute as quickly as he could. He recalled thinking the parachute jump was "going to pull all my insides out." McWherter landed on the ground and crashed into position. His sergeant, who had jumped after him, landed on his feet, bounced once, grabbed his shoes, and unfastened his parachute buckles while McWherter was struggling to untangle himself from his parachute straps and stand upright. "Scared the hell out of me," was McWherter's only comment.

Around the same time as the parachute episode, McWherter met the young woman who was to become his wife. In Union City, a small town approximately twenty miles from Dresden, the Davy Crockett Hotel served as the local venue for business, political, and social gatherings. The Davy Crockett was built by Emery Beck in 1930. Five stories high, the hotel was the tallest structure in Northwest Tennessee and considered very modern, with one of the few elevators in that part of the state. When the Mississippi River would flood, as the river did with regularity before the Tennessee Valley Authority, evacuees from Kentucky and as far away as Mississippi stayed at government expense at the Davy Crockett Hotel. With Reelfoot Lake less than an hour's drive from Union City, fishermen and duck hunters used the Davy Crockett as their base. Between the sportsmen and the federal government, Beck was able to operate the hotel at a profit, even through the depression years. A lively and congenial host, he provided excellent food, superior service and late night card games for his guests. The hotel was famous for Davy Crockett Chess Pie, which was served from the day the doors first opened. Always attentive to his guests' special needs, Beck hired Benny Patterson as bell captain. Benny worked at the Davy Crockett as long as the hotel was in operation, from 1930 until the farewell dinner in 1977. One of Benny's special assignments was to secure alcohol for the hotel patrons during the prohibition years. McWherter referred to Benny as "the expediter of spirits."

Emery Beck and his wife Mary had a daughter, Bette, born on May 15, 1929. Attractive and congenial, Bette would frequently accompany her friends to the Brown Derby restaurant in nearby Fulton, Kentucky. The Brown Derby in the early 1950s was well-known in Northwest Tennessee as a "classy place." Although the restaurant did not have a license to serve alcohol, patrons were encouraged to bring their own bottle in a "brown bag." A frequent diner at the Brown Derby, McWherter met Bette there in 1952. They subsequently dated, or rather "had a courtship," as McWherter described the relationship. Bette had been married previously and had a three year old daughter, Linda. Later that year, McWherter and Bette Beck were married in the Methodist Church in Bette's home town of Union City. The new family moved into a duplex in Dresden on the Paris Highway. Later they rented a home in town near Dresden Elementary School before eventually building a small house on Parkway Street. Several other young couples moved into new homes on Parkway Street around the same time. They dubbed the street "Mortgage Row." In 1956 Ned and Bette's son Mike was born.

Over time, Bette developed a dependency on alcohol. She and Ned separated. Despite the separation, Bette and McWherter's mother remained close, with Miss Lucille frequently helping Bette care for Linda and Mike. Bette eventually overcame her struggle with alcohol, but in 1973 she developed breast cancer and died soon thereafter, at age forty-four. For the entire time Bette fought breast cancer, Miss Lucille remained her constant nurse. After Bette's death she assumed the rearing of the two McWherter children.

By the late 1950s Ned had left Bay-Bee Shoes and taken a sales job with an independent shoe company in Sheffield, Alabama. His work throughout the South kept him on the road all week, leaving on Monday morning and returning late on Friday evening. The shoes were poor quality, or "junk," in McWherter's words. The company soon declared bankruptcy. Back in Martin, seven miles north of Dresden, two local entrepreneurs saw an opportunity and bought the bankrupt company. Jack Vincent was Martin's mayor and the local Falstaff beer distributor. Paul Clark owned the Pepsi-Cola bottling distributorship. Vincent and Clark arranged to transfer the equipment at no cost from Alabama to Martin. They renamed the business the Martin Shoe Company and began manufacturing shoes. They also hired McWherter as a salesman. The Martin Shoe Company line was equivalent to a lower priced version of Bay-Bee Shoes. Even though The Martin Shoe Company's product was inferior in quality to Bay-Bee's, the line sold well and the company produced close to 10,000 pairs each week. A new retail outlet, Dollar General Stores, was gaining popularity, especially in a number of southern states. McWherter received an order from Cal Turner, head of the discount chain. The Martin Shoe Company appeared to have found an anchor customer.

As the relationship blossomed, McWherter bought stock in Dollar General. Years later, McWherter was invited to a Dollar General Stores board meeting and watched a film about the history of the discount chain. A small black child's boot was prominently displayed in the board room, one of the shoes McWherter had sold to Turner in the early days of Martin Shoe Company. Holding the shoe over his head, Turner announced to his board, "Ladies and gentlemen, this is the boot I bought from the Governor of Tennessee." McWherter laughed and asked Turner if he could have the boot "to take home." Turner honored the request. Today the boot resides in the Ned McWherter room of the Weakley County Library.

Although the library was built with money provided by McWherter, he gives credit for the building to Cal Turner and Dollar General Stores. Soon after McWherter first started doing business with the chain, Dollar General went public with an initial stock offering for ten dollars a share. McWherter "scrounged up and saved seven hundred dollars and bought seventy shares." He later invested an additional thousand dollars in Dollar General Stores, and, over the years, reinvested any dividends in additional stock. When McWherter left the Governor's Office and wanted to build a library in Dresden, he sold his shares of Dollar General, which by then had a market value of $299,000. He "threw in another $50,000" to make the library a reality. McWherter insists the facility should really be called the Dollar General Library.

Even though Martin Shoe Company was securing a number of accounts, McWherter observed that marketing and retail strategies were changing drastically as a result of cheap imports from countries such as Japan. Martin Shoe Company could manufacture children's sandals for $1.10 to Dollar General Stores, which sold them for $1.98. The price was affordable to customers and provided a satisfactory profit to the Martin Shoe Company. Competition intensified when the Japanese began importing the now ubiquitous "flip-flops" into the U.S. market. Flip-flops sold for much less than the Martin Shoe Company sandals—ninety-nine cents, then forty-nine cents and sometimes as low as twenty-nine cents. Despite the fact the Japanese imports were not as sturdy as the Martin Shoe Company's sandals, customers were swayed by the price. Since they could not lower their costs, Martin Shoe Company's challenge, and thus McWherter's challenge, was to find new markets for their product.

In search of customers, McWherter began attending shoe conventions in New York City. Although he had traveled extensively throughout the South, he had never traveled to New York, and like most southerners was a little unnerved by his initial trip to Manhattan. "The first time I went to New York City, I was young and had no idea what to expect. I flew up there on a four-engine Eastern Airlines plane. I stayed at an old hotel and rented a room to show our shoes." Without a budget that allowed him to rent both a display room and a bedroom, McWherter relied on his ingenuity. During the day, while the shoe show was in progress, he pushed three tables together in his hotel room, draped a sheet over them, and displayed his wares. At night he slept on a rollaway bed he had tucked under the display tables. "I simply didn't have the money to do any different."

In New York McWherter did business with older, more experienced shoe salesmen. Seeking to disguise his youth, he rubbed talcum powder into his sideburns to turn his hair gray and, hopefully, convince customers he was a veteran salesman. Oddly, within six months his hair began to lighten on its own. He later wondered if wishing he looked older actually made his hair turn grey. More likely the gray hair was simply his family's genes at work. Miss Lucille's hair turned gray while she was still a young woman. Whatever the reason, McWherter's hair turned almost completely gray while he was still in his thirties. Looking back, he bemoaned the fact that his experience "up North" did age him, but he also states emphatically that "It was in New York that I learned how to survive."

McWherter encountered salesmen from all over the world at the New York shows. As a result, he soon branched out, seeking a new market for his shoes in the Caribbean. He had little success peddling his sandals in pre-Castro Cuba, even though he made four trips to Havana. He also sought markets in Santo Domingo and Panama, to no avail. He even traveled to the backwater of British Honduras in search of distributors. He sold few shoes, but he left with a remarkable anecdote.

"I went to Belize, British Honduras, cold, with no contacts, trying to sell shoes. It started to rain...hard...as it frequently does there. Near the Ft. George Hotel there was a little tin roofed bar, with an open front and a long table. I ducked in and ordered a beer. A man sat down next to me. He was from Louisiana and had moved to Belize to supervise a big farming operation. We got to visiting back and forth and I told him I was from Tennessee. The man's name was George Broussard. Eventually, George left British Honduras and ended up just down the road from Dresden in the little community of Sharon, where he married a local woman named Glenda Lee. Twelve years later, after I was in the legislature, I happened to be at the Weakley County Country Club in Sharon and I looked up and it was the guy from British Honduras. The man said, 'I know you. You stood under that tin roof in Belize that day in the rain.' Funny things happen to you in this life."

McWherter finally struck gold in San Juan, Puerto Rico. The Martin Shoe Company established a warehouse in San Juan and partnered with a Puerto Rican named Pete Palos. McWherter spoke no Spanish. Palos, who was fluent in both Spanish and English, took McWherter under his wing, introducing him to the businessmen and the culture of Puerto Rico. Palos represented several name brand shoes lines, including the well known Genesco brand, but at the time he and McWherter met, Palos had not found a low cost children's shoe. After examining McWherter's product line, he decided to distribute a particular Martin Shoe Company children's sandal called Sturdy Step. The sandals were made by a process called "compo," with the sole glued rather than stitched to the upper part of the shoe. Palos lined up several jobbers who sold Sturdy Step shoes on commission. Twice a year, Palos and McWherter would travel throughout Puerto Rico, filling orders.

McWherter would fly to San Juan each January and collect orders from Palos and his island distributors. The Martin Shoe Company shipped the merchandise to Puerto Rico throughout the winter and spring. In July, McWherter would again make the trip to Puerto Rico, collect the money for the January sales, and start the process again. Payment was sometimes in the form of checks, but just as likely could be "cash money." The transactions eventually forced McWherter to pick up a little Spanish, but only because of a major mistake. Palos had ordered two thousand pairs of Mary Jane girls shoes and requested they be black patent leather. McWherter mistakenly wrote "bianco" on the order form. Naturally, the shoes arrived in San Juan a bright, shiny white. The Martin Shoe Company, and McWherter, had to eat the order. The near disastrous experience convinced

McWherter he had better learn at least enough Spanish to conduct business.

In yet another of the life-forming experiences, the trips to Puerto Rico also taught McWherter how to interact with people who were different from Northwest Tennesseans. Over the years he often told a harrowing story about one of his early trips to San Juan. He and Palos once scheduled a meeting with a jobber in the village of Ponce, across the mountains from San Juan. Today the trip would entail no more than a fifteen minute plane ride. In the early 1960s, the only way to reach Ponce was by car. The trip took four to six hours in a hot car across narrow mountain roads.

McWherter and Palos concluded their business with the jobber around nine o'clock in the evening. They headed back with $30,000 in cash. Suspecting they might be robbed on the road back to San Juan, Palos recommended that he and McWherter split the $30,000 but keep only a couple of twenty dollar bills in their wallets. Palos instructed McWherter to remove his sock, cram his half of the $30,000 into it, put the sock back on, and wedge his foot, money and all, into his shoe. Palos did the same.

As they had feared, while Ned and Palos were rounding a sharp curve near the crest of the mountain, three "banditos" armed with rifles stopped them. McWherter and Palos got out of the car with their hands up. The banditos opened the yellow leather shoe sample cases, searching for cash. Palos explained in rapid Spanish that he and the Gringo were "poor salesmen" and had only enough money to cover their expenses. Unconvinced, the banditos proceeded to force McWherter and Palos to place their billfolds on the hood of the car and back away. The banditos took the cash from the wallets, which, thanks to Palos' advice, contained only about seventy dollars. None of the bandits thought to check the socks. After the banditos took the cash, they returned the empty wallets to the "poor salesmen," thanked them politely, and vanished. McWherter and Palos returned to San Juan without further incident. Looking back, McWherter quipped, "On that trip I learned that you really can sock money away."

On one of McWherter's other Puerto Rico trips, Jack Vincent, co-owner of the Martin Shoe Company, accompanied him. Vincent was Mayor of Martin and, during his tenure, brought natural gas and the first telephone switchboard operation to the city. Vincent had political clout and business acumen, but did not own either a suit or a set of teeth. In preparation for the trip to Puerto Rico, Vincent bought a sixty dollar blue and white seer sucker suit. Vincent disapproved of belts and hitched his pants up with suspenders, or "galluses" as they were then called. Vincent offered to travel with McWherter to Puerto Rico to check out a business opportunity, but had never flown and was leery of air travel. Vincent was also tight fisted. Rather than fly from Memphis to Miami, and then on to San Juan, as McWherter usually did, Vincent insisted the two of them drive Vincent's old Ford as far as Miami. They thus avoided the plane as long as possible and, of course, saved money. In Miami, they boarded a flight to Puerto Rico, which at that time took six and a half hours.

The plane took off just before midnight and landed as the sun was breaking over the Caribbean. McWherter and Vincent landed in a fierce rainstorm. They descended the steps from the plane, each carrying their luggage— McWherter with one suitcase and a shoe sample case and Vincent with no personal luggage but two sample cases. They remained in the downpour as they hailed a taxi at the airport. By the time a cab stopped both were soaking wet. Vincent's seer sucker pants had started to "draw up his legs." McWherter recalls that Vincent was sporting white socks. "We stayed in Puerto Rico four nights and five days and Jack wore the same clothes the entire time." McWherter, however, could not say a word about his suit. Vincent was bankrolling the entire trip.

Vincent's behavior on that memorable trip stood out as much as his wardrobe. McWherter and Vincent traveled to the small mountain community of Cedra to meet a jobber, who lived in a lovely, traditional Spanish style home with a red tile roof. McWherter knew from previous trips that the jobber was a gracious host and would no doubt offer them a cocktail before lunch and explained to Vincent what to expect upon their arrival at the jobber's villa. Vincent was a diabetic and had to monitor his diet carefully, especially if alcohol was involved. As they approached the villa, McWherter and Vincent passed a farmer walking beside the road carrying a large bunch of bananas over his shoulder. As their car passed the farmer, Vincent yelled, "Stop! Stop!" He leaned out the window, pulled three bananas off the stalk, and handed the man a dollar bill. The stunned Puerto Rican proceeded to place the entire stalk of bananas in the back seat of the car. McWherter remembers, "Jack ate them damn bananas the whole time we were in Puerto Rico."

In May, 1962, Madelyn Bradberry, the little girl whose father owned the Donut Shop in Dresden, graduated from high school. She enrolled in Union University in Jackson, with the intention of becoming a nurse, but withdrew after only one semester. In December she entered Bruce's Business College. During the winter of 1963, her dad became critically ill. Raymond Bradberry died in May. McWherter knew Madelyn needed a job, but feared that working together might destroy their lifelong friendship. He met and "talked long and hard" with Madelyn and her mother, Mattie Lee. Afterward, he hired Madelyn, then nineteen, on a three-month trial basis, with the agreement that she complete her business courses by attending classes at night. McWherter paid her twenty-four dollars a week.

The three months passed. McWherter said nothing about her continuing. Madelyn finally worked up the nerve to ask if she was going to keep the job. McWherter peered over his tortoise shell reading glasses and dryly commented, "Well, you're still here, aren't you?" And after forty-four years she still worked with McWherter every day, in her words, "still doing the job I was doing when I first started. I wouldn't change a thing."

They shared an office and one telephone at the Martin Shoe Company. A Warm Morning stove issued the only heat. The money McWherter earned in commissions he immediately used to buy stock in the Martin Shoe Company. Madelyn performed the secretarial work, kept the books, and prepared the freight bills. McWherter had become a partner in the company, although he continued to work as a salesman.

A year after Madelyn joined McWherter at the Martin Shoe Company, she married George Pritchett. The ceremony took place in November 1963, the weekend after President Kennedy was assassinated. Their only son, Brad, was born in 1974.

McWherter characterized Madelyn's role: "She's always been responsible and efficient and loyal. She always conducted herself in a proper way and, more than anything else, I could depend on her. She's very knowledgeable and knows more about my business than any other person. I always told her if I suggested she do something and she felt uncomfortable, not to do it and tell me about it. On occasion she has followed that advice. From an investment standpoint, she's been known to say 'You ought to take another look at that. It doesn't look right.' And I've always followed her advice. She is absolutely amazing."

The early days in the rough and tumble shoe business led McWherter to develop strong beliefs about how people should be treated. "That was a tough business," he said. "It's tough being in a business where you can't get enough mark-up in your product to give your employees a decent wage and benefits." McWherter vowed that whatever his next business venture, he would make sure he could pay his employees decently, provide good benefits, and give them something to look forward to when they retire.

After his separation from Bette, McWherter built a small garage apartment behind his parents' home on the corner of Evergreen and Cedar streets in Dresden. On Easter Sunday morning, 1962, faulty wiring in the attic of his parents' home caused a fire. Madelyn remembered sitting in the Dresden Methodist church when she heard the sirens. They sounded right at the end of the Easter service and "everybody fell out of church and went to the fire." Everything in the house was lost with the exception of a tall oak china cabinet with a curved glass front and claw foot legs. The fire spread to the garage apartment. McWherter's furnishings, his business files and his clothes were destroyed. Because of his size, Ned had never been able to walk into a department store and purchase suits or even shirts off the rack. His clothes by necessity were custom made. After the fire, Madelyn's father Raymond Bradberry measured him for clothes to replace those that had been destroyed. Until the clothes arrived, McWherter each day wore the suit he had on in church that Easter Sunday morning.

McWherter was not destined to remain a shoe salesman. Using the counsel of his old friends and mentors with his own vision and business sense, in the mid-1960s he developed the enterprises that would make him a wealthy man. His start came from Jack Vincent. Through his contacts in the beer industry, Vincent learned that Anheuser Busch was reorganizing and seeking new wholesalers in the South. Vincent suggested that McWherter consider seeking an Anheuser Busch distributorship in Northwest Tennessee. The current distributor had crossed swords with Anheuser Busch and consequently was removed from the beer business. McWherter met with the Anheuser Busch representatives at the old Biltmore Hotel in Union City and entered into negotiations. All McWherter needed was twenty-five thousand dollars to buy out the current distributor's business, which consisted of a forklift, one old truck, two manual typewriters, a wooden stool and eleven thousand dollars' worth of inventory. He approached local banks for a loan, but he was turned down because Northwest Tennessee bankers did not believe investing in a "beer joint," as they termed the deal, was a good risk.

McWherter turned to an old friend of his parents, Carlos Brundige, from Latham. Brundige was not a polished man, but he was savvy and had acquired a quiet fortune. Some thought Brundige was the wealthiest man in Weakley County, although nobody knew his exact worth. He owned thousands of acres of timber, which he harvested and processed at his saw mill. McWherter explained to Brundige his plan for the Budweiser distributorship. Brundige advised him to "talk to Mr. Vaughn at Peoples Bank in about a week. If he won't give you the money, I'll see if I can get it up." A week later, McWherter and Vaughn got together and, "against his better judgment," Vaughn loaned him twenty-five thousand dollars. He informed McWherter the only reason he granted a loan for "a beer business" was because Carlos Brundige had convinced him it was a sound business decision.

Then as now, Northwest Tennessee was a conservative area. Bankers were not the only people anxious about McWherter launching a beer distributing business. Miss Lucille, who still attended the Church of Christ, was uneasy with the prospect of her son going into the beer business. Sensitive to his mother's concerns, McWherter took her to the site of the distributorship to inspect the operation first hand. When she understood McWherter would not be selling beer but only distributing it, she said, perhaps a little hesitantly, "I guess it'll be all right."

Madelyn remembered the occasion distinctly. She "took a letter" for McWherter, her very first attempt at shorthand. The letter was a request to August Busch, President of Anheuser Busch Brewery, for the rights to the Busch distributorship to include Weakley, Henry, Benton, Obion and Carroll counties in Tennessee. On January 20, 1964, the corporate papers were signed and the company that was to become Volunteer Distributing opened its doors. McWherter was the sole proprietor. Madelyn Pritchett kept the books. M. L. Higgs was the warehouse man. Jack Moore drove the only truck.

Dresden was a dry town, meaning that liquor and beer were not sold in any public establishments. McWherter had no intention of changing the status quo. The distributorship supplied private clubs, the local American Legion Post, the Dresden Elks Club, and some "beer joints" scattered around the rural areas of Weakley County. McWherter, in a process of rationalization, never really considered himself in the beer business, but rather in the trucking business. Throughout his career he remained proud of his businesses and designed his corporate office in Dresden to be a place where people could come to gather and enjoy themselves.

From the modest beginning, McWherter, along with Madelyn and Jim Crews, established Eagle Distributors, which marketed Country Club and Strohs beers, both brewed in Detroit. Neither brand sold well in Northwest Tennessee. After three years they sold the operation's assets to Dixie Distributors in Jackson, but kept the corporation and converted it to an investment company. Today Eagle Distributors only has three stockholders—McWherter, his son Mike and Madelyn Pritchett.

McWherter continued to seek advice from more experienced businessmen. Judge Cayce Pentecost once told him that he should get into the nursing home business "... because there is a lot of future in it." McWherter heeded the advice and arranged a meeting with Eddie and Mary Ellis, who managed the Weakley County nursing home. The three consulted the judge's son, Cayce Pentecost, Jr., an attorney, about a possible location for a private nursing home. Cayce Pentecost, Jr. had purchased a fifty-five acre farm during World War II as an investment, but never developed the property. The story around Weakley County was that Cayce, Jr., who flew DC 3's during World War II, had spent his R&R playing poker, was pretty good, and sent his winnings home to his father. Cayce Sr. invested the money in land, and by the time the war ended, the younger Pentecost was left with a sizable piece of farm land.

McWherter bought the property from Cayce, Jr. for $12,000 on a six-year land contract. Along with Pentecost and Eddie and Mary Ellis, McWherter organized a company and began planning a nursing home. They approached Roy Overton, chairman of the Martin Savings and Loan and applied for a loan of $100,000, the most money McWherter had ever borrowed. Allan Strawbridge, Sr., a Dresden attorney, sat on the board of the Savings and Loan and Strawbridge encouraged the board to grant the loan because he also believed in the financial potential in nursing homes. McWherter was awarded the loan. He remembers Roy Overton, the chair of the Savings and Loan, telling him, "That's what this savings and loan was created for—to help the community. Ned, I'm willing to take a chance." Their confidence paid off. The nursing home became a reality on September 16, 1966. Eddie and Mary Ellis administered the facility and Madelyn worked as the secretary and bookkeeper. Mary and Eddie Ellis began with a combined salary of fifty dollars a week. They managed the nursing home until their retirement in 1993. They were able administrators and paid close attention to the needs—and wishes—of the patients.

Although the facility conformed to state health regulations, common sense sometimes required that the regulations be bent just a little. McWherter regularly ate lunch at the nursing home. His grandmother lived there, as did many elderly people he had known since his childhood. He enjoyed visiting them and listening to their stories. One Friday morning after returning from Nashville and his work with the legislature, he strolled in around eleven o'clock and sat at the "family table" back in the kitchen. He glanced over and noticed Edna, the cook, had piled a huge stack of English muffins on the back of the big industrial stove. McWherter asked, "What in the world are you going to do with all of those English muffins?"

Edna huffed, "The state dietician said we needed English muffins, but the patients here don't have any teeth and they can't chew them. They want biscuits and gravy, so here the muffins sit. I baked them but I'm not going to serve the residents something they can't and won't eat." McWherter recalled the incident every time he ate an English muffin. More important, he learned that people are most comfortable with the culture in which they grew up, and that government needs to be flexible enough to respond to those differences. McWherter became adept at understanding people's needs and priorities because he took the time to understand their environment.

Madelyn related that McWherter's ease with people enabled him to make friends easily and contributed to his success as a businessman and public official. "When he worked at the shoe factory, he was constantly going up to people, shaking their hands, putting his arm around them, talking to them. He knew them by name and would ask about their kids. He was genuinely interested in them and their families. He's done the same thing with each company he's formed. Each is like family. If something happens to one of us, everybody chips in and is concerned, and Ned is the first to help. He cares, and when he walks up and puts that big arm around you it's like everything's going to be all right."

Carlos Brundige, the family friend who helped McWherter with his foray into the beer distributorship, was also instrumental in helping establish a transport company called Volunteer Express. McWherter had a friend in Dresden named Jimmy Wharton whose father hauled gas and diesel fuel to Weakley County from Memphis during World War II. Wharton served in the Navy during the war, and after returning to Dresden he took over his father's company, Wharton Transports. Carlos Brundige contracted with Wharton Transports to haul lumber and believed the company was sound. McWherter approached Brundige about a loan to buy an interest in Wharton Transports. Brundige agreed. McWherter drove to Latham where he and Brundige sat on a log, drew up the terms of the $7500 loan on the back of a brown paper sack, and signed the deal.

Wharton Transports grew into an operation of approximately thirty units that hauled petroleum products, asphalt and bulk clay. When McWherter eventually sold his interest in the company to Jimmy Wharton's family, he retained one truck and one tank. He first used the truck to haul gas to the Weakley County Oil Company. He subsequently bought an additional five trailers and three trucks and gained the rights to haul general commodities from Weakley and Obion Counties to Nashville. Volunteer Express was born. The bookkeeper was Madelyn Pritchett.

As his parents aged, McWherter felt the restaurant business was becoming too much for them. Wanting to make their lives a little easier, he again approached his old friend Carlos Brundige for a loan to buy a Cities Service distributorship in Dresden. Harmon and Miss Lucille operated the station, working on a strict commission, with their income dependent upon the amount of gas sold. While the work may have been easier in a physical sense, Harmon and Miss Lucille missed the restaurant and the daily interaction with their patrons. After a few years, McWherter sold the distributorship to Sam Bone and Terry Oliver. Harmon and Miss Lucille became the resident managers of the Davy Crockett in Union City, the hotel Bette Beck McWherter's father constructed in 1930. Bette had inherited the hotel upon her father's death. When Bette died the property passed on to Linda and Mike, Ned and Bette's children. Harmon and Miss Lucille administered the Davy Crockett until the hotel was sold and converted into efficiency apartments for senior citizens in the mid 1970s. Madelyn Pritchett, as she did with all of McWherter's enterprises, handled the finances.

As his business ventures widened and his reputation in West Tennessee grew, local business leaders and politicians began to approach McWherter about a possible run for the Tennessee legislature. Cayce Pentecost, Sr. and Robert "Fats" Everett had whetted his appetite for politics years earlier, but McWherter had never sought public office. Back in 1950, when Ned was only twenty years old, he drove Everett's car during the Tennessee congressman's bid for office, taking the candidate to barbecues and chitterling suppers throughout Weakley County. McWherter was too young to vote, but he "licked stamps and drove the candidate around," and the friendship forged back in 1950 continued until Everett died. McWherter credits Everett with being his first political mentor. Everett was finally elected to the U.S. Congress 1958. Because he had helped in Everett's campaigns, McWherter and his wife Bette were invited to attend the inaugural ceremonies in Washington, D.C. The visit was McWherter's first to the nation's capital.

McWherter made a serious turn to politics in 1968. He was thirty-eight and still working at the shoe factory when Doug Murphy, who succeeded Jack Vincent as mayor of Martin and owned the local funeral parlor, approached him about running for the Tennessee legislature. McWherter initially turned him down, thinking his selling trips to Puerto Rico and the Southeast would make a campaign difficult. Murphy argued that McWherter might be able to run unopposed since the incumbent, Milton Hamilton from Obion County, was a candidate for the state Senate. Jack Vincent weighed in and helped persuade McWherter to give it a try. He finally acquiesced with the understanding that he run unopposed. He was elected to the 76th legislative district as a Democratic candidate representing Weakley and Obion counties. Many Tennesseans never realized that in eighteen primary and general elections for the state legislature, McWherter faced opposition only one time, a fact that seems certain to have had an impact on his willingness to undertake a statewide race. The simple walnut desk and chair that Ned occupied in the Tennessee House of Representatives sit in the Weakley County Library.

When later asked about the secret to his success, McWherter gave a characteristically simple answer. "My parents and the people I came into contact with growing up gave me the foundation to be successful, and I took it from there."

He was grateful to Harmon and Miss Lucille who taught him to value truth, honesty and hard work, but who also taught him that life should contain a fair portion of fun. McWherter told the story about his mother's reaction to folks' comparing her son with Dan Blocker, the actor who played Hoss Cartwright on the 1960s television program "Bonanza." Many thought McWherter and Blocker had more than a passing resemblance, both in looks and size. McWherter, Al Gore, Sr., and Blocker once had their picture taken together. One of Miss Lucille's friends saw the photo and commented that McWherter and Cartwright looked like they could be brothers. Miss Lucille retorted, "Oh, no, Ned's much prettier."

If his parents instilled his basic values, Ms. Valda Stewart gave him the self-confidence to mingle as comfortably with the President of the United States as with the farmers at the feed store. His Future Farmers of America advisor, V. J. Shanklin, provided him with the parliamentary skills to become an effective Speaker of the House of Representatives. Tom Reagan convinced him to stay in school.

Once he entered the business world, McWherter became fascinated with the strategies of simple men for doing things well. He was generous with the praise of his Weakley County mentors and credits them with much of his success. "What I know about finances I learned from Paul Clark, the Pepsi-Cola bottling distributor, who taught me how to read *The Wall Street Journal* and how to understand the stock market, bonds, convertibles, and ventures. Old Cayce Pentecost and Jack Vincent taught me always to look to the future and evaluate challenges that present themselves. Mr. A. L. Drerup taught me how to go out into the market place and sell your product. He told me, 'When you go out selling shoes, you've got to keep going, even if you don't make a sale.' That's what it's all about—you just keep going. You develop a relationship and people gain confidence in you."

Doug Murphy and Judge Cayce Pentecost, Sr., convinced McWherter to enter public service. Perhaps most influential of all was Carlos Brundige, who was McWherter's financial backer when nobody else had the confidence to loan him money. McWherter described Brundige as "one of those very quiet men. He ran a saw mill and he owned land and he made tremendous investments. He was a person I relied on when things got tough or when I saw an opportunity. I would go to Latham and sit down on a log. Mr. Brundige would only talk a little while, because he was always working the saw and needed to keep it running. He understood numbers, whether the numbers were large or small. He gave me money when others wouldn't let me have it. Most of the time, he would say, 'Come back in two or three days and I'll see if I can get some money together.' And he did."

If McWherter had one regret, it was the lack of a college education. He understood early that he would have to work hard, often harder than others, because of his lack of education. "Ten years after I got out of high school I realized I made a mistake by not going to college. I realized I'd have to work longer and harder and do some things I probably wouldn't have had to do to be successful. If I'd been able to speak Spanish, I could have done even more when I was in the Caribbean. If I had a degree in business, I could have gone into the banking business in Puerto Rico. I had to overcome my lack of education by hard work and lots of effort."

By 1969, McWherter had overcome any handicaps that resulted from not attending college. With good instincts and hard work, he had created financial security. The mold was cast. At the age of thirty-eight, the people who touched his life had prepared him for a far greater challenge that was just beginning.

THE LEGISLATIVE YEARS

1969-1986

PART TWO

THE LEGISLATIVE YEARS

1969-1986

Although McWherter may not have realized it when he took the oath of office as a state legislator for the first time in January 1969, Tennessee state government was on the verge of historic changes. Much of the national political debate in the late 1960s was focused on race relations, urban violence and a widespread dissatisfaction with the Democratic administration's handling of the war in Vietnam. The 1968 presidential bid by George Wallace of Alabama had given expression to the frustration of many Democrats, especially in rural West Tennessee, who for the first time in a half century began in large numbers to part from traditional voting patterns and vote for independents or Republicans.

As national forces propelled a shift in state politics, other factors also were transforming the political landscape in Tennessee. Suburban communities in Shelby and Madison counties, as well as the bedroom communities surrounding Nashville, were rapidly becoming dominated by young middle class white families, many of whom were the first generation with a college education and the promise of long term prosperity. For many of these families, the tensions that accompanied integration in their schools and neighborhoods outweighed traditional loyalty to the Democratic Party. These demographic shifts coincided with the emergence of a new generation of more sophisticated Republican candidates seeking to take advantage of the dissent within the ranks of Tennessee Democrats by running for local and statewide office.

If McWherter did not anticipate fully the scope of the political changes underway, he certainly was aware of their impact on the General Assembly when he took his seat in the last row of the House chamber in 1969. For the first time since Reconstruction, Republicans, bolstered by a surge of victories in Shelby County, held an even number of seats with Democrats in the House of Representatives. With the support of the body's single independent member, the Republicans elected Rogersville attorney Bill Jenkins as Speaker by a vote of 50-49.

McWherter's first legislative term coincided with the final two years of Governor Buford Ellington's administration and the end of a gubernatorial dynasty that began with the election of Frank Clement in 1952. The two rural Middle Tennessee Democrats had served alternate terms in the Governor's Office for eighteen years. First elected at age 32,

Clement was a captivating orator who defined the standards for personal campaigning and local political organization. More reserved and less charismatic, Ellington had forged his political base during his tenure as executive director of the influential Tennessee Farm Bureau, a fact not lost on McWherter.

The most significant legislative event of McWherter's freshman term was Tennessee's decision to participate in the federal Medicaid program. Designed to provide free medical care to indigent mothers and their children, Medicaid represented in both financial and philosophical terms a historic expansion of Tennessee government's commitment to provide social services. Though McWherter voted for the new $39 million program, he stated years later that he and many other legislators who supported Medicaid's intent privately had expressed grave reservations about its long term implications for the state budget. As he would come to realize two decades later, the reservations were justified.

The 1970 elections marked the culmination of forces unleashed by the Wallace campaign in 1968 and resulted in the emergence of the Republican Party as a full equal to the Democratic Party in Tennessee. While Tennessee voters had provided slight majorities for Dwight Eisenhower and Richard Nixon in their presidential bids, Howard Baker had been the only successful Republican candidate for statewide office in a half-century. Correctly sensing a possible defection by thousands of rural and suburban Democrats, Republicans nominated a respected East Tennessee congressman, Bill

Brock of Chattanooga, to run for the United States Senate. For Governor, they nominated little known Memphis dentist and former Shelby County Republican Chairman Winfield Dunn.

At the very moment when Democrats needed to close ranks in the name of party unity, the party seemed intent on self-destruction. Governor Ellington refused to support his party's candidate for governor, flamboyant Nashville attorney John J. Hooker. Incumbent Senator Albert Gore's outspoken opposition to the war in Southeast Asia made him an easy target for Republicans who appealed to Tennesseans' sense of patriotism. The result was a catastrophe for the Tennessee Democratic Party. For the first time in modern history, Republicans occupied the Governor's Office, both senate seats and a majority of the congressional delegation.

The shock that lingered from the Republican sweep formed the context of McWherter's second legislative term and his first bid for leadership within the Democratic Party. Ironically, the Republican tide in the statewide elections did not extend to the legislative races, where Democrats regained control of the House of Representatives. Democrats elected as Speaker Nashville lawyer Jim McKinney, a fiery partisan who made little pretense of cooperating with the new Republican governor. McWherter was elected Chairman of the House Democratic Caucus.

Prior to Dunn's election as governor, the notion that Tennessee state government contained three equal branches did not exist outside the official Tennessee Blue

Book. The Legislature had few staff available to analyze budgets or legislation proposed by the administration or various lobbying groups. Legislators came to Nashville only a few weeks each year and worked out of their rooms across the street from the Capitol; Republicans at the Hermitage Hotel and Democrats at the Andrew Jackson Hotel. With rare exceptions, legislators rubber-stamped administration proposals with little or no debate. On occasion the State Budget passed on the House and Senate floors without amendments in less than two minutes.

The conflicting agendas of a Republican governor and a highly-partisan House speaker led to repeated clashes. Dunn sought to transform in wholesale fashion the priorities and patronage of state government. McKinney was equally determined to thwart any Republican initiative, regardless of its merit. Partisan exchanges became increasingly personal and bitter. Public decorum on the House floor deteriorated to the point that McKinney sometimes cut off the microphone of legislators who dared challenge him.

In a now famous meeting that took place one summer evening in 1972 on a house boat near Nashville, a number of House Democrats, their confidence bolstered by beverage, urged McWherter to challenge McKinney openly and run for Speaker. Beyond a distaste for McKinney's abrasive style, a combination of reasons motivated most of those present. Some correctly assumed that a new speaker would provide those who supported him a chance for more rapid advancement to leadership positions. Others simply wanted to see the House rid itself of the political divisiveness that was jeopardizing progress in Tennessee. Each legislator was aware that the consequence of defeat was political oblivion. Late in the evening, McWherter accepted the nomination of the rump caucus and agreed to challenge the House Speaker.

The impact of the McGovern presidential campaign fiasco in 1972 extended to Tennessee, where the head of the ticket carried only a handful of the most Democratic counties. Republicans Richard Nixon and Howard Baker rolled to large reelection majorities. More important for McWherter, several of the Democratic legislators he had counted on for support were defeated. Not only was his nomination by the Democratic caucus in serious doubt; the Democrats were reduced to a precarious majority of 50–49 in the House.

The 1973 race for House Speaker became perhaps the most famous in Tennessee history. Despite efforts by McKinney both to woo and intimidate undecided legislators, McWherter prevailed by a single vote in the House Democratic Caucus. Sensing a wedge among the Democrats, Governor Dunn attempted to use the considerable resources of the executive branch to entice a single Democrat to defect and support a Republican candidate for Speaker. Rumors spread throughout the Capitol that he had succeeded, and in fact as late as midnight before the vote it appeared that Dunn might have the commitment of a black Democrat and McKinney supporter from Nashville. With McKinney presiding under the House rules during the vote, McWherter was elected

Speaker by a vote of 50-49. A new era in Tennessee politics had begun.

The House Speaker in 1973 had a small staff consisting of a secretary and a Chief of Staff who coordinated, in addition to legislative issues, the activities of the Chief Clerk, the Engrossing Clerk and the Sergeant at Arms. McWherter selected as his first Chief of Staff Jim Free of Columbia. Free was immediately introduced to his new job when, as he tried to enter the Speaker's Capitol office after McWherter's election, McKinney's wife slammed the door on his fingers. From this inauspicious beginning, Free in time became Chief Clerk for McWherter and eventually head of legislative affairs for President Jimmy Carter.

McWherter's first act as Speaker was to solidify his base within the Democratic Caucus by rewarding those who at considerable risk had supported his challenge to McKinney. As Speaker, he was authorized by the House rules to assign both the membership and the officers of each standing committee. To the consternation of Republicans, McWherter broke Tennessee precedent by awarding all committee leadership positions to Democrats. He next reorganized the Committee on Calendar and Rules by structuring its membership from the officers of the respective standing committees, in effect making the committee one composed entirely of Democrats. At McWherter's direction, the House rules were amended to require that before consideration on the House floor, every bill must receive a recommendation for passage from the Committee on Calendar and Rules as well as the appropriate standing committee. With these changes, McWherter was able to consolidate enormous power, move control of this power into the Speaker's Office and thus set the stage for a dramatic realignment in the relationship between the executive and legislative branches.

McWherter's next move was to embark upon a strategy designed to shatter the unity of the Republican Caucus and place Governor Dunn on the wrong side of an issue important to much of his political base in East Tennessee. For some time, a bipartisan coalition of elected officials and business leaders in Northeast Tennessee had lobbied for the establishment of a new state medical school at East Tennessee State University in Johnson City. The group's most prominent and influential spokesman was Republican Congressman Jimmy Quillen of Kingsport. The group pointed out that while some Tennessee communities had one doctor for every 500 residents, other counties in Northeast Tennessee had fewer than one doctor for every 7,000 residents. They argued persuasively that the presence of a regional medical school would result in more doctors and improved medical care for the area's rural communities.

Governor Dunn openly opposed Quillen's proposal on grounds that Tennessee could not afford and thus could not justify a second state medical school in Johnson City. While Dunn's argument had merit, the fact that the Governor had graduated from the existing University of Tennessee medical school 500 miles away in his hometown of Memphis made him vulnerable in East Tennessee to claims of regional favoritism. Tensions between Dunn and East Tennessee Republicans escalated. Legislative debate and editorial commentary increasingly became personal attacks on the Governor.

To Dunn's astonishment, the Democratic Speaker from West Tennessee entered the dispute on the side of the East Tennessee Republicans. Over the Governor's strenuous objections, the General Assembly passed legislation to establish and fund the new medical school in the final days of the 1973 session. The apparent legislative victory was the most significant in more than a generation for residents of Northeast Tennessee. Area newspapers hailed the beginning of a new era for a region that had long perceived itself neglected by state government. Shortly after the Legislature adjourned for the year, the unthinkable happened. Governor Dunn vetoed the bill.

The Governor's veto landed like a mortar shell in Northeast Tennessee. Congressman Quillen publicly likened Dunn to Benedict Arnold. Newspapers ran viscous front page cartoons with similar themes. An already volatile situation turned violent when Dunn attempted to locate a prison in nearby Morristown. Opponents cut down power lines and dug trenches to halt prison construction. Dunn refused to back up on either issue. By the time the General Assembly returned in January, any hope of compromise had evaporated.

The effort to override Dunn's veto in the winter of 1974 took on a significance far broader than the debate about the medical school. In the final year of his term, the

Governor viewed the fight as a legislative referendum on his administration and a validation of his leadership. In only his first term as Speaker, McWherter saw an opportunity to realign the political forces of the Legislature and establish himself as the leader of a more aggressive and co-equal legislative branch of government.

Proponents of the medical school never doubted their ability to prevail in the Senate. The showdown was to be in the House, where the Governor leaned hard on the Republican Caucus and made it clear he was prepared to trade with any interested Democrats. In public McWherter appealed with equal intensity to the emotions of rural legislators who were sensitive to the health care needs of the state's underserved communities. In private he also laid out clearly the political consequences for the Democratic Party and a Republican Governor if Dunn could be defeated on an issue of such emotional importance in his East Tennessee base.

On the day of the override vote, many thought the outcome was in doubt. McWherter convened the House believing that he had the votes. As McWherter looked up from the Speaker's podium, he saw Memphis Mayor Henry Loeb standing in a trench coat, motioning to him from the back of the chamber. As McWherter later recounted the brief conversation, Loeb threatened "to destroy McWherter's career" if the Speaker went through with attempts to override the veto. With the help of several West Tennessee Democrats, the House passed the veto override by a single vote.

Eleven years later, McWherter was invited to deliver the commencement address at the graduation ceremonies of the East Tennessee State University Medical School. With great effect, he recounted Henry Loeb's threat and the momentous decision he confronted as a freshman Speaker in 1974. Raising his voice and breaking into a broad smile, McWherter observed that as a result of that decision, he was still Speaker of the House, while Henry Loeb was last seen selling farm equipment in Forrest City, Arkansas. The faculty and graduates gave McWherter a standing ovation.

With a one-vote election victory as Speaker and another one-vote victory on the veto override, McWherter's high profile victory over Dunn solidified his role as Speaker and catapulted him among the leaders of the Tennessee Democratic Party. For the next twelve years, his strategy appeared a paradox to many in both parties. He annoyed the Republican leadership by continuing to stack the Calendar & Rules Committee with Democratic committee officers. On rare occasions he used the Committee to block legislation, usually to send a message to an individual legislator or to an interest group that had steamrolled a bill through a standing committee. While using his Democratic committee officers to establish an effective bottleneck with the Calendar & Rules Committee, McWherter simultaneously consolidated and expanded his influence in the House by bringing into his bi-partisan coalition East Tennessee Republicans grateful for his assistance with the medical school. He reorganized and strengthened the campaign arm of the House Democrats. A more disciplined strategy of campaign fundraising and organization resulted in an increasing Democratic majority in the House. Even as Democratic influence grew, however, McWherter included both Democrats and Republicans in budget decisions and issued a personal pledge that for the first time every legislator would be granted a hearing on any piece of legislation. To the consternation of some Democrats, he refused to use the reapportionment process in 1981 to redraw Republican districts. As a result of this outreach to the Republicans, McWherter was consistently able to secure 20-25 Republican votes, even on the most controversial issues.

Another secret to McWherter's effectiveness as Speaker lay in a cultural phenomenon that was evident only to those closest to the legislative process. McWherter's original base of support in the House came from rural West Tennessee Democrats. In the early 1970s, this group included virtually all the legislators between Memphis and the Tennessee River. With few exceptions over the years, the group's members had a remarkable similarity. All shared an uncompromising fiscal conservatism that was balanced by a legacy of Jacksonian populism. The West Tennesseans also shared a genuinely sophisticated sense of humor, often laced with barnyard language, that could be brutally effective in a closed-door political debate. They would bicker among themselves, but usually close ranks in support of a colleague believed to be threatened by Republicans or special interests.

McWherter organized the legislators into the West Tennessee Caucus, which met every Tuesday morning in the Speaker's office to discuss legislative strategy. At night, while Middle Tennessee legislators went home and East Tennesseans divided into various cliques, the West Tennesseans gathered in the "Caucus Room," a non-descript room off the garage of the Downtowner Motor Inn across the street from the Legislative Plaza. With a juke box, bologna and crackers, and plenty of beer and wine, they socialized together each night while they planned their legislative strategy. Years of this camaraderie among the West Tennesseans produced friendships and political loyalties that simply cannot be appreciated by those who were not a part of the group. McWherter, although he did not participate in all of the social activities, was acutely aware of the talent and political potential of the West Tennesseans. Over time the original group produced a governor, House Speaker Jimmy Naifeh, and Congressman John Tanner. Quietly and without drawing attention to the group, McWherter used his role as Speaker to give expression to the values of his fellow West Tennesseans and in turn used their support for his agenda.

In pursuing his agenda, McWherter made it difficult to assign an ideological label to his political philosophy. In the 1970s, for instance, one of the General Assembly's most contentious issues involved the ability of the state's teachers and state employees to organize associations authorized to negotiate contracts and lobby on their behalf. Most Republicans, almost reflexively, were opposed to the efforts of both groups. In two particularly high-profile legislative fights, McWherter sided on behalf of the State Employees Association to fund their activities through a payroll deduction plan, and with the right of teachers to negotiate annual contracts collectively with individual school systems. In each case, however, he firmly opposed the right of either group to strike. In this context, he was viewed by many groups as "pro-labor" and simultaneously by much of the business community as supportive of their interests.

McWherter's role in major policy decisions expanded in 1975 with the election of West Tennessee Congressman Ray Blanton as Governor. Blanton had been elected by surviving a field of ten candidates in the Democratic Primary with some 22 percent of the vote. In the general election he defeated young Maryville Republican Lamar Alexander, a protégé of Howard Baker whose country club image did not sell well in the rural counties of Middle and West Tennessee.

Blanton's administration proved to be one of the most corrupt in Tennessee history. Plagued by alcoholism, Blanton was often detached from his duties and his staff, several of whom sought to use their offices for financial gain through the sale of pardons, liquor licenses and surplus state property. Many who worked with Blanton state that he acted responsibly in the mornings until he started drinking around lunch. The alcohol produced a crude personal style and an undisguised contempt for the press that made his term as Governor a period of constant controversy. In an act that characterized his arrogance and lack of judgment, Blanton announced during a drunken live television interview that he would pardon an inmate recently convicted of double murder and the son of a political supporter. The public indignation that followed this announcement doomed any remaining chance Blanton had for a productive relationship with the press and the General Assembly.

A 1977 amendment to the Tennessee Constitution made it possible for Blanton to seek a second term. All but the most fervent Blanton supporters acknowledged the obvious, and Blanton announced in the spring of 1978 that he would not seek reelection. Though his name was floated as a potential candidate, McWherter did not feel the timing was right for a rural West Tennessee Democrat to follow Blanton.

With McWherter on the sidelines, the Democratic nomination in 1978 went to Knoxville banker Jake Butcher, who defeated Bob Clement, son of former Governor Frank Clement, in a close and divisive primary election. The Republican nomination once again went to Lamar Alexander, who reshaped his image by walking from Mountain City to Memphis in a red-checked flannel shirt.

The Butcher-Alexander race set new standards in Tennessee campaigns for spending. McWherter campaigned actively for Butcher, but privately was put off by Butcher's ostentatious wealth, his tendency to be late for events and his inability to develop a campaign message. In contrast, Blanton's corruption gave Alexander a simple and appealing theme. What appeared for a time to be a close race by election day became a rout for Alexander.

Blanton's judgment and behavior continued to deteriorate during the weeks following the 1978 elections. After Alexander's victory in November, Blanton became increasingly more strident in his contempt for public opinion. In the days leading up to Alexander's inauguration, Blanton announced that as his last act he would pardon dozens of inmates, many of whom were incarcerated for serious crimes. The Governor's office drafted a stack of some fifty pardons with Blanton's signature and submitted them for certification to the office of the Secretary of State.

Faced with an irresponsible act that threatened a public firestorm, the state's political leadership decided to undertake an unprecedented action. On Wednesday evening, three days before the scheduled inauguration, McWherter joined Senate Speaker John Wilder in the Tennessee Supreme Court Chamber to issue the oath of office as Governor to Alexander. FBI agents occupied the Governor's Capitol office, confiscated files and changed the locks, bringing to an end one of the darkest chapters in modern Tennessee history.

The corruption and embarrassment associated with the Blanton Administration obscured at least one important accomplishment that occurred during his term in office. Under the leadership of McWherter, Finance Commissioner Bill Jones, State Treasurer Harlan Mathews, State Comptroller Bill Snodgrass, House Finance Committee Chairman John

Bragg and Senate Finance Committee Chairman Douglas Henry, Tennessee quietly put in place a series of fiscal policies that produced lasting benefits to state government. The state's retirement fund became one of only a handful in the nation to be fully funded, aided by a new legislative Council on Pensions and Retirements that blocked unsound attempts to tamper with the fund. The Legislature established a cost-effective program of scheduled maintenance for state facilities including higher education. The Legislature further strengthened Tennessee's financial reputation by enacting a statute that required ten percent first year funding of all state bond authorizations.

These and other similar policies reflected a deep fiscal conservatism on the part of McWherter and his colleagues that extended beyond rhetoric. The actions were not glamorous in the traditional political sense and thus received little attention from the press and the public. The policies were noticed, however, by the Wall Street financial markets, which awarded Tennessee a AAA bond rating that over time produced enormous savings in the form of lower debt service.

The extraordinary circumstances under which Lamar Alexander moved into the Governor's Office shaped much of his approach to governing during his first term. After the embarrassment of Blanton, many Tennesseans asked only that the new Governor be honest and tasteful. Alexander responded with a series of public relations moves that sharpened his contrast with Blanton and built upon

Tennesseans' need to restore respect for the Governor and pride in the state. The new Governor played the piano with local symphonies. He conducted "community days" in which he would make a brief appearance in his trademark red-checkered shirt to help paint a church or school. He took an active role in the National Governors Association. Though one could argue that some of these activities were examples of style over substance, they were well-received by a majority of Tennesseans eager to feel good about themselves and their Governor. Alexander's personal popularity soared.

Alexander's first term is not remembered for an aggressive legislative agenda. He responded to public disgust with Blanton by introducing a crime package that removed the Tennessee Bureau of Investigation from the executive branch and established longer prison sentences for what Alexander labeled "Class X" crimes. Alexander's frequent use of labels and props became the subject of closed-door humor for legislators and the media. Annual budgets were called "Bare Bones" or "No Frills" proposals. Likewise, legislative initiatives were labeled "Healthy Children," "Safe Growth" or "Master Teacher." Many legislators privately made fun of what they felt was Alexander's preoccupation with the media. They also grudgingly conceded that Alexander's public relations efforts were more sophisticated and more effective than those of any Tennessee Governor in memory.

McWherter's relationship with Alexander proved to be a crucial factor in Alexander's considerable

Born in Weakley County, McWherter spent his early teenage years in Michigan, where his father moved to work in a bomber factory during World War II. His mother worked in a White Castle restaurant.

When winter storms froze the dirt roads, McWherter's father would put three or four children on a horse and walk them to the one-room school in Little Zion.

With his high school football coach. A good athlete, McWherter "wore out the door" going in and out of the school's academic honor club.

1947 Dresden High School football team. McWherter, 2nd row, 4th from left, hurt his knee playing football. The injury prevented him from playing in college.

Ned and Bette McWherter
in the office of Congressman
"Fats" Everett. After a traditional
"courtship," the two married and
set up housekeeping on "mortgage
row" in Dresden. Bette died
of cancer prior to McWherter
becoming Speaker.

Lucille McWherter. Probably the
greatest influence in McWherter's
life, his mother wanted him to be a
doctor. His teenage goal was to be
a highway patrolman. She lived to
see her son sworn in as Governor.

Speaker McWherter with son Mike in the House chamber. Mike McWherter campaigned actively for his dad in 1986 and eventually took over much of the family business.

Family portrait. Standing from left, Steve Ramsey, Matt Ramsey, Linda McWherter Ramsey, Brett Ramsey, Ned McWherter, Walker McWherter, Mike McWherter. Seated, Mary Jane McWherter and Bess McWherter.

House Speaker McWherter greets Governor Winfield Dunn at the State of the State address. Although personal friends, McWherter's defeat of Dunn on efforts to build a new medical school at ETSU launched his career. *Tennessee Library & Archives*

Early swearing-in of Lamar Alexander as Governor after fear that out-going Governor Ray Blanton was preparing to pardon dozens of felons. From left, Alexander, Speaker McWherter, Honey Alexander, Attorney General Bill Leach, Secretary of State Gentry Crowell, and Chief Justice Joe Henry. *Nashville Banner*

Also from rural West Tennessee, Governor Ray Blanton was never close to McWherter. Although plagued by scandal, Blanton's Administration joined with the legislative leadership to put in place conservative fiscal policies for state government.
Tennessee Library & Archives

Sharing a laugh with Lamar Alexander. Bipartisan cooperation between the West Tennessee Democrat and the East Tennessee Republican contributed to passage of Alexander's education initiatives.
Tennessee Library & Archives

Tennessee National Guard summer camp at Fort Stewart, Georgia, with Adjutant General Carl Wallace. A guard veteran, McWherter as Speaker visited with the Tennessee troops each summer. He received strong support from the Guard in his 1986 race for Governor. *Tennessee Library & Archives.*

Betty Haynes, left, and Madelyn Pritchett were both long time personal assistants. Haynes adeptly managed the hundreds of administrative details during McWherter's tenure as speaker and Governor. A childhood friend, Pritchett managed a variety of his Dresden business affairs since the age of nineteen. *Tennessee Library & Archives.*

House Speaker Pro Tempore Lois DeBerry of Memphis was one of McWherter's most valued confidants, both as House Speaker and as Governor. As a young freshman legislator, the urban DeBerry introduced herself to the rural Speaker by walking into his office and sitting on his lap. *Tennessee Library & Archives*

Rural West Tennessee Power. The friendship revealed in this photo with Senate Speaker John Wilder and House Speaker Jimmy Naifeh was genuine. A protege of McWherter, Naifeh's skills as Majority Leader and later as Speaker played a key role in McWherter's success in the Legislature. *Tennessee Library & Archives.*

success with the Legislature. The partisan nature of his committee assignments belied the fact that McWherter was fundamentally uncomfortable with the idea that partisanship needed to accompany every issue or decision. Although substantial Democratic majorities in the House and Senate would have made it possible to block Republican proposals and reek havoc with the state budget, McWherter genuinely believed that the good of the state required the Legislature to be "responsible"—a word he used repeatedly— and extend cooperation to the Governor. Except for minor upward adjustments in recommended state pay raises, legislative changes to Alexander's budgets during his first term were few and relatively insignificant. With McWherter's support, the Legislature enacted most of the Governor's proposed legislation, though little was noteworthy.

Aside from restoring a measure of pride lost during the Blanton years, Alexander's most important achievement during his first term was the cultivation of a close relationship with the Japanese corporate community. Tennessee was the first southern state, and among the first in the country, to court Japanese investment aggressively. The relationship culminated in 1982 with the announcement that Nissan Motors would build a manufacturing plant twenty miles south of Nashville in Smyrna. Nissan's $500 million investment represented the first major car manufacturing plant in the South and the largest single investment in Tennessee history.

Overnight, Tennessee was transformed from an economic backwater to a player in one of the world's most highly visible industries. Nissan's commitment to Tennessee was followed by a number of automotive supplier plants, many of them Japanese. By the time General Motors decided three years later to locate its new Saturn plant thirty miles from Nissan in Spring Hill, the automotive industry had produced a historic shift in the Tennessee economy. As apparel manufacturing declined across the state, low skill jobs in shirt and shoe factories were replaced by higher skill and higher wage jobs building cars, tires and a variety of automotive components. How Tennessee responded to this shift would become an important part of McWherter's political philosophy and would shape his political future.

Alexander's 1982 reelection effort was less a campaign than a celebration of the new image he had brought to Tennessee. The state's leading Democrats, including McWherter, were intimidated by the popularity of the young Republican Governor and chose not to run. A weak Democratic field produced a replay of the 1978 Butcher-Clement primary with stand-in candidates. Knoxville Mayor and Butcher confidant Randy Tyree defeated Senator Anna Belle Clement O'Brien, sister of the late Governor Frank Clement and aunt of the defeated 1978 candidate, Bob Clement. Tyree prevailed in a contest in which neither camp was well-funded or well-organized.

Tyree's general election campaign never enjoyed the financial or emotional support from most Tennessee Democrats who, like McWherter, did little more than go through the motions. Despite heavy financial backing from

Jake and C. H. Butcher, Tryee's campaign never got out of first gear. Meanwhile, Alexander, who also received funding from the Butchers, benefited from the attention showered on Tennessee during the 1982 World's Fair in Knoxville. Although the World's Fair was organized and funded largely by the Butchers, Alexander succeeded in using the Fair as further evidence of Tennessee's newfound confidence and influence. On election day Alexander clobbered Tyree by the largest Republican margin in Tennessee history.

Alexander's second term was as active and ambitious as his first term was cautious. His reelection campaign had given no indication of a proposal that would become the most controversial since the medical school issue a decade earlier. In keeping with his instinct for public relations, Alexander in early January announced his initiative on statewide live television in an address to the Tennessee Press Association. Called the Master Teacher Program, his plan called for a Department of Education assessment of teachers that in turn would provide salary supplements of $1,000 to $5,000 for those evaluated as "Master Teachers." The plan would be funded by a one cent increase in the state sales tax.

Alexander's proposal immediately encountered emotional opposition from the Tennessee Education Association, which espoused the basic belief that it is impossible to discriminate fairly among average and outstanding teachers. (TEA never conceded that a category of substandard teachers existed.) TEA's skepticism toward Alexander's initiative grew with news that the plan had been developed by Chester Finn, a Vanderbilt professor widely known for his frequent criticism of public education. TEA registered 56 lobbyists from local school districts and gave them simple instructions: "Do not compromise. Defeat the bill."

To counter TEA's expected opposition, Alexander engaged in a public relations blitz unlike any before witnessed in Tennessee. In dozens of speeches before business and civic groups, he provided a simple prop and an effective one-sentence description of his plan that stuck in the public consciousness. Holding up a penny, he would dramatically begin each speech, "In Tennessee, not one teacher is paid one penny more for doing a good job." Thousands of Tennesseans who had little idea how Alexander's Master Teacher Program would work nonetheless became convinced that it was a good idea.

The broad statewide support that Alexander generated for the Master Teacher Program did not immediately translate into votes needed for passage in the General Assembly. The Democratic leadership quickly determined that a crucial bottleneck for the legislation would be the Senate Education Committee, comprised of five Democrats and four Republicans. The swing vote was Senator Anna Belle Clement O'Brien. The Clement organization had clandestinely supported Alexander in 1978 in retribution for what they felt was a vicious assault by Jake Butcher in the Democratic primary. In 1982, however, TEA had given Anna Belle O'Brien $20,000 and considerable logistical support in her losing primary bid. Both sides put tremendous pressure on O'Brien. When the roll was called before a packed hearing room, O'Brien repaid her debt to TEA and voted to defer the Master Teacher legislation for one year.

After a brief period of casting blame, Alexander came to realize that despite his considerable public relations skills, he could not pass the legislation without McWherter's help. The Governor invited the Speaker to his retreat at Blackberry Farms near Knoxville. After dinner, on the porch as the sun faded over the Smoky Mountains, Alexander told McWherter that the future of Tennessee education was in the Speaker's hands. In his West Tennessee vernacular, McWherter replied that it was unfair for Alexander to frame the issue in such personal terms. The Governor persisted. McWherter finally agreed to lend his support with the understanding that substantial changes in the legislation would be necessary.

Alexander worked tirelessly through the summer and fall to build public support. Meanwhile, a select legislative committee held hearings on the issue of performance-based salaries for teachers. Significantly, the committee's executive director was on loan from McWherter's staff. Working closely with Alexander's Chief Counsel Bill Koch and Education Commissioner Robert McElrath, the committee staff rewrote major portions of the original bill. Finally, by an 8–7 vote, the committee recommended a merit pay plan to the General Assembly.

McWherter's major contribution to the legislation (now referred to as the "Career Ladder") was what became known as the "Weakley County Amendment," named for McWherter's home county. The new version made teacher participation in the Career Ladder optional subject to a positive evaluation for tenure after the fourth year. Evaluation teams were modified to include a local teacher in addition to two state evaluators. Despite these changes, TEA did not endorse the legislation and fought it at every juncture with dozens of amendments and parliamentary maneuvers.

In January 1984 Alexander intensified the debate by calling the General Assembly into Special Session for the express purpose of considering the Career Ladder and the one cent sales tax. Press support for the proposals was unprecedented. With McWherter's assistance, Alexander's education proposal steadily gained momentum. In early February, the Career Ladder legislation passed the House by a vote of 62–37. The Senate followed suit a week later.

As expected, the toughest hurdle for Alexander and McWherter was passage of the sales tax increase. The bill received 19 votes in the Senate, two more than the 17 needed for passage. Only McWherter's personal lobbying secured an eventual 52 votes in the House. With help of the rural West Tennessee Democrat Speaker, the East Tennessee Republican Governor had established a national reputation as a leader in education.

Time would prove that much of the Career Ladder program was flawed, partly because in 1984 the absence of desktop computers made it impossible to manage by hand the massive amounts of data required for thousands of teacher evaluations. Though ultimately of marginal education value, the program served to enhance Tennessee's image and provided a lasting contribution to the educational credentials of Alexander, who after his terms as Governor held posts as President of the University of Tennessee and U.S. Secretary of Education.

By the passage of the education reforms in 1984, Governor Alexander and Speaker McWherter were clearly established as the leading political figures in state politics. The two represented a dramatic contrast in style. Born in one of East Tennessee's most Republican counties, educated at New York University, Alexander played classical piano and moved at ease with Tennessee's intellectual and cultural elites. From rural West Tennessee's Democratic stronghold and with only a high school education, McWherter rose from a hard-scrabble youth and identified closely with the culture of Tennessee's numerous rural communities.

The bipartisan cooperation between two leaders of such different backgrounds resulted in part because each, in a fascinating way, instinctively understood the other. In McWherter's case, political attitudes in Tennessee's rural culture are often rooted less in ideology than in simple notions of common sense, basic courtesy and respect that outsiders do not appreciate. One of the best examples of how behavior can shape lasting attitudes took place during Alexander's administration in a famous episode involving

Sam Donaldson of ABC News. In 1976, Speaker McWherter appeared on stage at a campaign event in Memphis in support of Presidential nominee Jimmy Carter. Covering the event, Donaldson instructed his cameraman to locate their tripod in front of the seated McWherter. The Speaker moved, whereupon Donaldson again moved the tripod in front of McWherter. Irritated, McWherter admonished the cameraman to "make up your mind where you want that Kodak." Donaldson glanced toward McWherter and instructed the cameraman, "Don't mind him, he's a nobody."

Six years passed. In 1982, President Ronald Reagan was scheduled to speak in the Tennessee House Chamber. Because the speech was Reagan's first since he was shot in a failed assassination attempt, coverage by the national media was extraordinary. The event was to be held in the House chamber, meaning that by protocol all decisions surrounding who could enter the chamber were at McWherter's discretion. (When the White House hurriedly attempted to contact McWherter in Dresden to arrange a formal request to use the House chamber, the secretary was informed by the Speaker that he would be out "fencing" that afternoon. The White House secretary, with the classic name of Ms. Peachie, asked McWherter if he would give her the phone number of his country club. The cultural gap could not have been greater as McWherter patiently explained that his cows did not have phones.) On the evening before Reagan's speech, McWherter reviewed the official list of press credentials and noted the name of "my old friend Sam Donaldson." McWherter quietly took a pen and placed a line through Donaldson's name. The next day, the White House press entourage stormed up the Capitol steps and jammed against the single door to the House chamber, where Chief Sergeant-at-Arms Greg O'Rear, the former Director of the Highway Patrol, checked names and allowed entry one by one. At six-foot nine and about 300 pounds, O'Rear was an imposing figure. When Donalson pushed his way forward, O'Rear informed him his name was not on the list and that he would either have to sit in the balcony or leave. Donaldson responded with a string of profanities and demanded entry. With the press corps watching, O'Rear announced in his bullfrog voice, "Mr. Donaldson, I have tried to ask you in a nice way to leave. If you don't leave, I'm going to have to ask you another way." To the great amusement of his colleagues, Donaldson stormed off and returned to Washington on a commercial flight.

Repeated a thousand times in the following years, the story put into focus McWherter's fundamental beliefs about courtesy and honor. The Democratic Speaker extended every courtesy to a visiting Republican President, a practice he later continued as Governor whenever a President, Democrat or Republican, visited Nashville. At the same event, however, McWherter did not hesitate to embarrass publicly one of the media's leading figures whom he believed was guilty of insulting both him and Tennessee. As Governor, Alexander understood and respected this rural mindset better than most.

In the midst of a campaign trip for Republican legislative candidates, Alexander's car approached the Weakley County line. The Governor immediately ordered the driver to stop and turn the car around, declaring he would not campaign in the district of the Speaker who had helped him win passage of his education package. Such courtesy was valued in West Tennessee, and explains at least to some extent the bipartisan cooperation that characterized the working relationship between Alexander and McWherter.

Alexander's public popularity after his high profile Career Ladder victory in 1984 was cemented a year later by another signature industrial investment. Some three dozen states had competed fiercely to attract a billion dollar investment by General Motors to build a new line of automobiles called Saturn. GM's announcement that Tennessee had prevailed over a number of other high profile competitors underscored the state's emergence as the South's leader in the automotive industry. To many in the national press, GM's choice of Spring Hill also established Alexander as a new kind of southern Governor who successfully marketed education and industrial development. The fact that Alexander's education initiatives did not address the funding inequities of rural school systems largely escaped notice. Likewise, the glamour of the Nissan and Saturn investments obscured a growing gap between Tennessee's prosperous counties and those that suffered from structural employment and declining personal incomes.

Alexander's ability to capitalize on the themes of education and new jobs also served to deflect attention away from the most serious shortcoming of his administration. After decades of relatively little growth, Tennessee's prison system began to feel the pressure from a dramatic increase in crime that began in the 1970s. A state that had constructed only two new prisons in 40 years suddenly had to build three during the Blanton administration. The crime rate continued its upward trend after Alexander's election in 1978, with the impact on the prison system exacerbated by the new Class X sentencing laws. Despite three new prisons, overcrowding worsened. Inmates at the Main Prison were triple-bunked in the prison gymnasium, with 2,000 prisoners packed into an eighty-year old facility built for fewer than 1,000. Throughout the system the old prison work program could not provide jobs for the growing numbers of new inmates. The combination of idleness and overcrowding produced a sharp rise in inmate violence. By 1982, the prison system was close to being out of control.

An administration that had devoted an extraordinary amount of energy to education and recruiting Japanese investment had assigned remarkably little attention to the problems of an increasingly violent prison system. Alexander's single attempt to address the problem—a hastily drafted proposal called the "Corrections Plan for the 80s"—was viewed by many as a half-hearted effort and lasted little more than a year. After an inmate riot burned several buildings at

Turney Prison in October 1985, the federal court stepped in and took over control of the Tennessee prison system.

Alexander's response was a textbook study of crisis management. He called the Legislature into a second Special Session in November to address the prison crisis. At the direction of the Federal Special Master, Alexander proposed to fund construction of two 500-bed maximum security facilities and renovate the remainder of the state's facilities. The price tag was $250 million.

Faced with few options, McWherter and the General Assembly grudgingly approved Alexander's proposals. Meanwhile, the Attorney General agreed to accept a long list of demands from the Federal Master rather than fight those demands that exceeded minimum constitutional standards. The consent agreement with the Court in effect removed the ability of the next governor to manage the prison system. The increasingly chaotic process in the state's corrections system was particularly annoying to McWherter, who by then was putting in place his campaign organization for the 1986 governor's race.

For a time, the corrections issue went away, at least from the front pages of the newspapers. Unfortunately for McWherter, from the day in November 1985 when the Legislature appropriated funds to build two new prisons until Alexander left office 14 months later, continued conflict with the Federal Court meant that plans for the new prisons remained, in effect, a blank sheet of paper. The neglect of this issue in 1986 by both Alexander and McWherter would prove to have lasting consequences.

In the meantime, McWherter was moving, cautiously and methodically, toward the third and most important chapter of his career. After serving as Speaker of the House longer than anyone in Tennessee history, he was ready, financially and emotionally, to apply all his skills and experience to the most challenging job of his life. But before he could test his talents as Governor, the man who had faced opposition only one time in eighteen elections had a final hurdle. He had to get elected.

THE CAMPAIGN FOR GOVERNOR

1985-1986

PART THREE

THE CAMPAIGN FOR GOVERNOR

1985-1986

By late 1984, McWherter was nearing a decision on whether to enter the race for Governor in 1986. After flirting briefly with the idea of running in 1978 and again in 1982, McWherter sensed that circumstances at last offered a more promising opportunity. Two terms under Alexander had energized Democrats across Tennessee eager to win back the perks and patronage they had surrendered to the Republicans. Since 1974, McWherter had laid the groundwork for a statewide race by gradually increasing his visibility and stature within the state Democratic Party. For fourteen years, he had regularly attended annual statewide meetings of the Farm Bureau, the Tennessee Education Association, the State Employees Association, and the Tennessee Labor Council. His nightly calendar always included "drop-bys" at the Nashville legislative receptions for the sheriffs, realtors, bankers and a host of other professional organizations. Speaking engagements at dozens of Rotary clubs and county Democratic bean suppers throughout the state extended his name recognition to those who knew little of legislative politics. Through his role as House Speaker, McWherter cultivated relationships with an array of interest groups, local officials and community leaders who sought his help with the legislative process. The majority of those who sought the Speaker's assistance left with positive feelings. To most, McWherter was viewed as helpful, a compromiser, and not, in his words, a "flag waiver."

With Tennessee's other leading Democrats, Senator James Sasser and newly-elected Senator Al Gore, attracted to the national stage, McWherter increasingly became the focus of attention from Democratic activists seeking a candidate of stature. Democrats in the state's congressional delegation were either too young, too old or too controversial to undertake a statewide race. Shelby County Mayor Bill Morris hinted publicly he was considering a race, but privately did not relish a primary campaign against a rural West Tennessean. None of the previous Democratic candidates—Bob Clement, Randy Tyree, and Roger Murray—was considered viable.

In addition to McWherter, two other prominent Democrats encouraged speculation about the Governor's race. Former congressman and three-time Nashville Mayor Richard Fulton made no secret of his desire to move his office up the street from the Metro Courthouse to the Capitol. Fulton was generally popular as Mayor and over his career had developed a strong relationship with the state's organized labor movement. Most observers predicted Fulton would appeal to elements of the Democratic Party's more liberal wing.

Also assessing her chances was Nashvillian Jane Eskind, a member of the Public Service Commission and the National Democratic Finance Committee whose personal wealth would make her—if not a favorite—at least an important factor in any Democratic primary contest. Eskind's obstacles were different from those of either Fulton or McWherter. Though a member of the PSC, she was not well-known. Also, she would be a Jewish candidate in a state with fewer than 100,000 Jewish citizens. Eskind hoped these problems could be overcome with a well-financed media campaign appealing primarily to urban women and blacks.

McWherter's first formal campaign meeting took place in November 1984. Invited to his suite in the Capitol Park Inn were State Treasurer Harlan Mathews, Secretary of State Gentry Crowell, along with Jim Kennedy and Billy Stair from his office staff. Also attending was pollster Harrison Hickman from the Washington, D.C. firm of Hickman-Maslin. The meeting produced three decisions. McWherter would file papers officially creating the Friends of McWherter Campaign. The campaign would hire Hickman to conduct a statewide poll aimed at assessing McWherter's popularity and name recognition and that of his potential rivals. Finally, the campaign would begin a low-key effort to raise at least one hundred dollars from each of the state's 95 counties. The decision to solicit funds from every county had ramifications beyond the obvious desire to demonstrate widespread support for McWherter. Over time, the "95 County" strategy evolved into a larger commitment that influenced policy as well as campaign decisions.

With Mathews as his leading fund-raiser, McWherter quickly raised the symbolic funds from all 95 counties, including a single $100 check from tiny Hancock County. Meanwhile, Hickman's poll provided a mixture of encouragement and concern. McWherter led all his potential rivals among likely Democratic voters. Morris was second, but with a base of support almost entirely within the Memphis media market. Fulton was third with a wider base that included pockets of support in Memphis and Chattanooga as well as Nashville. Eskind was a distant fourth.

McWherter's numbers had two warning signals. Despite nearly 13 years as House Speaker, two out of five Tennesseans had never heard of him. Moreover, he registered an alarmingly low level of support among black voters needed to defeat a Republican in the general election.

The McWherter campaign group feared that neither McWherter nor Morris could survive a multi-candidate primary race in which both competed for the West Tennessee vote. As Morris sent a variety of signals about his intentions, McWherter announced a major fundraiser to be held in March at the Opryland Hotel in Nashville. Scheduled some 20 months before the 1986 election, the fund-raiser represented both a risk and an opportunity. Failure to meet the fundraising expectations projected by the press, his friends or his opponents would reinforce doubts about McWherter's potential drawing power outside the Legislative Plaza. Similarly, a stronger than expected fundraising effort would serve two immediate campaign goals. Wavering candidates such as Bill Morris would be left with no uncertainty about McWherter's commitment to the race and the level of his financial support. Equally important, a host of activists, interest groups and others with their fingers in the political wind would be motivated to jump on the band wagon while there was still room.

The Opryland fund-raiser was a success that exceeded the expectations of most persons inside and outside the McWherter camp. Through a strategy developed by Mathews that rested in large part on the creation of local steering committees, the event raised more than $700,000, a sum at that time among the largest for a single event in state history. From that night forward, McWherter became in the eyes of the press the candidate to beat in the Democratic primary.

In the closing weeks of the legislative session following the March fund-raiser, McWherter developed a plan to build on his momentum. He hired a scheduler and a press secretary for the campaign and established a full-time headquarters on West End Avenue in an old house formerly owned by Nashville Mayor Beverly Briley. His son Mike, a recent graduate from Vanderbilt Law School, took time off to be a surrogate for his father at parades and other events. His daughter Linda accompanied Miss Lucille to a variety of receptions, often hosted in the home of supporters. McWherter's plan involved using the summer and fall to visit all 95 counties, beginning in Johnson County on the North Carolina border and slowly working his way west. The format was much the same each day. Depending on the county, McWherter would speak to 25–35 Democratic activists at breakfast and again at lunch. In between he would visit the local newspaper and radio station. At night, he would attend either a fund-raiser, an event designed to build the largest possible crowd, or both. At all such events the campaign made a special effort to invite local leaders of the Tennessee Education Association and the Tennessee Farm Bureau.

The trip throughout the summer and fall of 1985 was a learning process for both McWherter and the campaign. The entourage left Nashville in June for a two week trip to Northeast Tennessee. McWherter traveled in a van driven by Trooper Steve Browder and accompanied by Kennedy and Stair. Events were organized with a combination of direction from Nashville and legwork from local supporters and volunteer advance staff from the campaign. In an atmosphere more low key than twelve months later, the campaign could evaluate the talents, shortcomings and reliability of persons assigned to perform a variety of tasks. The organization likewise developed an ability to respond to unexpected problems, from a drunk at a fund-raiser to media requests, without the attention and consequences that accompany the final weeks of a statewide campaign. Perhaps most important, Speaker McWherter developed a more clear sense of what candidate McWherter needed to say and how he needed to say it. After dozens of such events, his speaking style improved and his message sharpened.

The summer and fall trip across Tennessee also provided another asset for the campaign that surfaced a year later. McWherter's strategy was to form local organizations that would not suffer from the hard feelings left over from previous campaigns. The most serious such tension remained between the Clement and Butcher factions, each of which viewed the other as traitors to the party in the bitter 1978 gubernatorial election. Leaders of the respective factions in some rural counties refused to sit in the same room together. In most state and local elections since 1978, the Clement and Butcher factions had chosen sides and fought it out. McWherter needed both factions and attempted in each county to identify a young campaign coordinator without previous ties to either group. He largely succeeded, and in so doing also enabled the campaign to broaden its appeal to independents and Republicans attracted to McWherter's message. In county after county, McWherter's personal request produced commitments of support from sheriffs, district attorneys and a variety of other local activists crucial to success in a primary election. These commitments were especially important in East Tennessee, where all the candidates were relatively unknown.

McWherter began his final legislative session in January 1986 with two goals. He sought first to avoid mistakes his opponents could exploit in the campaign. The second goal was out of character for a Speaker whose style over the years had been to sponsor few bills and concentrate on behind-the-scenes efforts to pass or defeat legislation. With considerable fanfare, McWherter introduced bills that would strengthen the state's DUI laws and establish a state-funded venture capital program designed to assist economically depressed counties. The DUI legislation was an effort to shore up McWherter's image among voters uneasy with his ownership of a beer distributorship in West Tennessee. The venture capital bill was a symbol of McWherter's desire to do something innovative to help regions left behind in Tennessee's economic growth. Both bills passed easily, though their practical impact proved minimal.

The biggest surprise of the 1986 legislative session and the issue with the most potential to influence the campaign was Governor Alexander's proposal to plan and finance a multi-billion road construction program. Most observers, including McWherter, had anticipated that after winning a bitter fight with the General Assembly over education reform Alexander would coast through his last year cutting ribbons and attending events associated with his much-ballyhooed Tennessee Homecoming '86. Alexander's proposal to raise gasoline and diesel taxes to finance a massive 15-year construction program was a shrewd political move. Throughout his campaign trip during the previous months, McWherter's most popular talking point had been just such a road program for the state's rural counties. He assumed the idea would be a solid campaign issue and the legislative focus of his first year as Governor. Having read the county newspapers, Alexander realized McWherter would be hard pressed to oppose an idea the Speaker himself had advocated for six months. The fact that Alexander's notion of where to build the roads differed from McWherter's made it no less difficult for McWherter to oppose the proposal without seeming petty or partisan. After some modifications in the way the program would be financed and a few changes in the proposed projects, the Legislature raised the gas and diesel taxes and approved Alexander's plan with McWherter' s support.

As the 1986 legislative session neared adjournment in May, the field for the governor's race had come into focus. Although McWherter's official announcement was set for June, he had been running unofficially for twelve months and was the first to run television ads. Dick Fulton announced for Governor in late spring with a sparsely-attended "parade" up Charlotte Avenue from the Metro Courthouse to the Capitol. Jane Eskind announced her candidacy with a press release, an early indication of a campaign that would be run almost exclusively through television. In late winter, a select group of wealthy Republicans had met in the board room of the First American Bank in Nashville to anoint as their candidate former Governor Winfield Dunn. The message was clear: other Republican candidates wishing to raise funds need not apply. Dunn announced his candidacy from the Capitol steps to a small crowd of fewer than 100 persons.

McWherter's approach to his campaign announcement was a sharp contrast to his opponents and indicated much about the experience, skill and aggressiveness of the McWherter campaign staff. The campaign leadership, headed by Jim Hall of Chattanooga, decided early to stage the formal announcement in Northeast Tennessee instead of Nashville or McWherter's hometown of Dresden. The choice sought to resurrect the area's lingering sense of abandonment by Winfield Dunn by underscoring the fact that McWherter came first, and not last, to East Tennessee. The McWherter campaign also sought to have an announcement that included crowds at six separate events across the state. The logistics of such an announcement were extremely complicated. Like the early fundraiser in 1985, such a plan had equal parts of risk and benefit. Part of the problem was addressed by having McWherter attend a rally on the courthouse square in Dresden on the eve of his announcement. The event attended by some 1,000 friends satisfied the need to hold a rural West Tennessee rally for McWherter's base vote without spoiling the symbolism of having the "first" announcement in the Tri-Cities. McWherter left immediately after the event for East Tennessee, where he slept in a 150 year-old farmhouse across the highway from Rocky Mount, Tennessee's first territorial capitol located between Johnson City and Bristol.

The most challenging leg of the next day's five-part announcement was the Rocky Mount event, scheduled for 7:30 a.m. The attempt to build a respectable crowd before breakfast on top of a mountain defied all conventional wisdom about political announcements. No one knew with certainty whether the event would draw fifty supporters or 1,000.

Every aspect of the event, from attracting media to providing food, was made more difficult by the time and location. Concerned about these and other details, the campaign sent three advance staff to the Tri-Cities for two weeks in preparation for the event. As the morning fog lifted, hundreds of cars made their way up the hill toward the cabin porch from which McWherter would address a crowd estimated at 800-900 persons. The sunrise announcement before a large and enthusiastic crowd made a perfect picture for the wire stories and an ideal backdrop for television reports carried statewide. Later airport stops in Chattanooga, Memphis and Knoxville drew respectable crowds. The day ended with a large rally attended by several hundred supporters in the ballroom of the former Hyatt Hotel in Nashville.

The McWherter campaign's successful announcement illustrated important differences among the four campaigns vying to win the Governor's race. Most obvious in the McWherter staff was the experience and skill needed to organize six well-attended events in a period of 24 hours. Also evident in the McWherter camp were creativity and a willingness to take risks, qualities that many, especially in the media, had not previously associated with McWherter's laid back style. Finally, the large crowds made clear that McWherter's organization, unlike the others, was capable of generating visible support outside of Nashville. While to some extent creativity and organization can always be purchased with enough money, few statewide campaigns ultimately succeed if managed by staff with little real campaign experience. In this crucial area, the McWherter campaign began the election season with an enormous advantage.

By early June, McWherter had a commanding lead in the polls over Fulton and Eskind. Fulton's campaign never gained traction. Drawn largely from his mayoral staff, the Fulton campaign appeared unable to develop a strategy for the candidate that took him beyond metropolitan Nashville. Schedules were changed at the last minute or canceled. Although a successful mayor, Fulton's knowledge of state issues was weaker than anticipated, a problem made worse by a rambling speaking style. His tendency to respond to every issue by talking about Nashville did not resonate well with voters outside the Nashville media market. Fulton's expected help from labor never materialized, due in large part to successful efforts by McWherter, working with AFL-CIO President Jim Neeley, to obtain a formal vote of neutrality by the Tennessee Labor Council in the Democratic primary. Fulton also suffered setbacks in Memphis, where expected black support defected to Eskind. Like many before him, Fulton was a good mayor whose efforts to run statewide were handicapped by a campaign organization that did not understand the diversity of Tennessee's political landscape.

By mid-June, Fulton's polling numbers had dropped to the low teens. Frustrated and bitter, Fulton departed from the high road and launched an all out attack on McWherter. His televisions ads attempting to depict McWherter's beer trucks were clumsy and ineffective. He suggested during a forum on nursing homes that problems in the industry were related to McWherter's ownership of a nursing home. In a press conference held in the Legislative Plaza, Fulton played the card that all insiders knew would be laid on the table by the first candidate who lost confidence in his or her campaign. Saying it reminded him of Nazi Germany, Fulton denounced a vote by McWherter in 1969 that would have provided for the sterilization of welfare mothers. Fulton's conduct came across as desperate and tasteless. McWherter defused the issue simply by saying he had made a mistake 18 years earlier. Within days, polling numbers for Fulton dropped into single digits. His chances of winning the primary were effectively over.

The immediate beneficiary of Fulton's misfortune was Jane Eskind. While her campaign organization was little better than Fulton's, Eskind's personal wealth made it possible to put her message on television constantly with enormous blocks of advertising. The influence of such advertising was evident in her steady rise in the polls during a three-week period in June when McWherter was off the air and Fulton was self-destructing. Driven largely by an ad that focused on her opposition to a proposed federal nuclear waste transfer facility in Oak Ridge, Eskind's numbers doubled from the low teens to the high twenties. Meanwhile, Eskind's personal campaigning was kept to a minimum. Eskind was an uncomfortable speaker and ineffective among crowds. Her campaign staff was incapable of organizing multiple events on a regular basis. While McWherter was scheduling six or more campaign stops daily, Eskind's routine rarely varied.

The typical Eskind campaign schedule was a morning flight to a town for a luncheon speech to a women's group followed by an immediate return to Nashville. In the background, her staff targeted black voters across Tennessee through a variety of legal and questionable expenditures.

As the primary entered the final thirty days, McWherter faced his most important decision to date. Constant attacks from his rivals, coupled with Eskind's blitz of the airways, had reduced McWherter's lead over Eskind to a margin that was too close for comfort. The McWherter campaign had stockpiled an ample number of negative issues which, through the power of television, could take the focus off McWherter. His dilemma was the likelihood that hard feelings resulting from such criticism would produce a replay of the infighting which had destroyed Democratic chances in 1970, 1978, and 1982. After considerable internal debate among his staff, McWherter chose to ignore the attacks from Fulton and Eskind. When his commercials resumed in July, McWherter's polling numbers inched back upward about two points each week.

The primary campaign's most noteworthy events occurred during three debates conducted in July. Like the fund-raisers and announcements, the debates became for the media a point of comparison judged as much by style and expectations as by substance. As a long time Speaker of the House, McWherter made it a point during each campaign speech and interview to stress his knowledge of state government and the fact that he would be a "first day" Governor. Such statements raised the expectation that McWherter should dominate a debate on state government issues. The fact that McWherter had rarely engaged in the give-and-take debate format while in the Legislature made little difference, either to supporters who wanted him to dominate the debates or to opponents who wished to set him up for a fall. McWherter's staff attempted to do what most staffs do for their candidate—fill him full of facts and figures right up to the moment he walked on stage. The mistake was one which those closest to him should have anticipated. The information overload made McWherter ill at ease and caused him to be stiff and tentative in the first debate. He committed no blunders, but also did not dominate his opponents to the extent that many predicted.

For the second debate, held on Sunday evening in Nashville, McWherter decided to forgo any kind of conventional preparation. He spent the afternoon at the Belle Meade Cinema eating popcorn and viewing the movie "Top Gun." That night he took his place in front of the television cameras relaxed and confident. Eskind stumbled on a question that revealed the female candidate did not understand Tennessee's abortion laws. Later in the debate, when Eskind challenged McWherter about his plans for rural economic development, he replied with a brutal simplicity that staggered Eskind. Beginning with the fact that he had been several times to all 95 counties, McWherter asked Eskind: "Jane, have you ever been to Hancock County?" Eskind appeared frozen for a full ten seconds before stammering a barely audible answer that she had never been to Hancock County. Eskind never fully regained her composure in the debate, and after the next morning's new stories never regained her campaign's momentum.

McWherter's major decision during the primary's final days was how much money to spend on television and how much to save for the general election. Fulton was spending every dime he had and more. Eskind was spending, overtly and covertly, an amount of money witnessed only in the wild 1978 campaign with Jake Butcher. Overruling his media consultants, McWherter opted to spend no more money on television than originally budgeted. His decision was influenced by one of the campaign's unanticipated turns when Fulton redirected his negative ads toward Eskind. Conceding privately he would not beat McWherter, Fulton's face-saving goal appeared to be a second place finish over Eskind. In the primary's most clever and effective ad, Fulton chided the Public Service Commission for raising the cost of using a payphone, ending the ad with a dangling phone repeating, "Ask Jane Eskind, ask Jane Eskind..." All but acknowledging defeat, Fulton spent the last two weeks of the election entirely in Nashville, understandably irked at McWherter's untimely boast that he would beat Fulton in his hometown. Fulton's last 48 hours were a bizarre effort to campaign non-stop without sleep, soliciting shoppers in grocery stores at 3:00 a.m. and speaking to surprised strangers at all-night diners.

The Eskind campaign entered the campaign's last week with a massive media buy and an attempt to maximize the black vote. The Eskind family had long provided financial support to Congressman Harold Ford of Memphis as well as a variety of black causes. For the Eskinds, the product of this association was a gross misunderstanding of the size and relative influence of the black vote. The Eskind campaign became increasingly focused on the black vote to the neglect of almost every other voting block. Much of the white liberal support Eskind had won in June drifted back to Fulton in late July. Attempting to counter Eskind's television blitz by making her wealth an issue, the McWherter campaign repeatedly noted the growing number of Eskind television ads and the "obscene" levels of Eskind's spending. In the closing days at a McWherter rally in Lebanon, derisive bumper stickers appeared urging McWherter to "Make Her Spend it All." The bumper stickers were as close as McWherter came to direct criticism of Eskind.

After a final campaign swing through his base in northwest Tennessee, McWherter returned to Nashville on election night. He set up operations in the Spence Manor, with a planned victory celebration in the ballroom of the downtown Hyatt Hotel. A detail largely unnoticed but appreciated by political insiders was the security provided McWherter by employees of Nashville Sheriff Fate Thomas, head of Nashville's most effective political machine. Early returns indicated a substantial McWherter lead, running some 15 points ahead of Fulton and 13 points ahead of Eskind. Fulton called McWherter around 9:00 with a stiff but polite concession. The McWherter staff became anxious for

Eskind's call, wanting to get their candidate on live television for his victory speech during the ten o'clock news. Voting returns had stabilized, with McWherter at 42, Eskind at 29 and Fulton at 26 percent. As time passed, anxiety turned to anger as Eskind family members continued to assure television reporters the race would change dramatically when votes from Memphis and Chattanooga were fully counted. Well after 10:30, McWherter received a concession call, not from Jane Eskind, but from her husband Dick. McWherter immediately drove to the Hyatt to accept the nomination before a cheering and largely drunk crowd.

The most imaginative and perhaps most effective single campaign event of the entire Governor's race occurred on a whim the day after the primary. During the first morning of his initial campaign tour in June 1985, McWherter had visited a small two-chair barbershop in Mountain City. The barbershop was operated by elderly identical twin brothers. While the twins proclaimed proudly they had never voted for a Democrat, they responded to McWherter's friendliness by promising a free haircut if he won the primary 14 months later. On impulse, McWherter gathered his staff and flew to Mountain City to claim his free haircut. The event, even on short notice, attracted a mob of local television and newspaper reporters from the Tri-Cities. In contrast to the barrage of television ads to which the state had been subjected, the political impact of a simple haircut was tremendous. McWherter immediately dominated the news on the first unofficial day of the general election. He did so while reinforcing his commitment to Northeast Tennessee and, in the eyes of many, underscoring his image as someone who would travel 300 miles to save money on a free haircut. The event's only downside came when the twins, caught up in the media attention, cut off virtually all of McWherter's hair.

McWherter's immediate task was a need to unify the Democratic Party after a spirited primary campaign. Despite all statements to the contrary, few candidates and campaign staffers can endure months of public and private criticism without resentment. The campaigns had agreed prior to the Tuesday election to hold a public unity luncheon the following Thursday in Nashville. Fulton and Eskind went through the motions of endorsing McWherter and encouraging Democratic unity. McWherter responded by publicly proclaiming that Fulton and Eskind would be given Cabinet posts in a McWherter Administration. While the mood of the McWherter camp and Democratic officials was generally upbeat, those close to the candidates could sense a strain, particularly from Jane Eskind and her family. A possible explanation surfaced in later reports suggesting Eskind entered election night actually believing she was going to win. According to these reports, Eskind may have been given misleading polling data from Patrick Cadell, a former pollster for President Jimmy Carter who had established a unique one-stop shop for candidates that included both polling and media consulting. Such an arrangement presented a risk for candidates. Decisions regarding the size and nature of media buys usually are driven by polling data. Because media consultants receive a financial share of each media buy, a candidate has reason to keep the relationship between pollsters and media consultants at arms length. In Eskind's case, circumstantial evidence indicated that in the campaign's last weeks Cadell may have provided misleading polling data in an effort to encourage the Eskind campaign to purchase an ever larger number of television ads when in fact the chances of winning had become remote.

McWherter escaped town with Harlan Mathews and his wife Pat for a few days rest. Upon returning, the most significant campaign task was organizing a statewide Unity Tour featuring McWherter, Eskind, Fulton, the Democratic congressional delegation and the Public Service Commission.

Meanwhile, the McWherter campaign for the first time turned its attention to Republican candidate Winfield Dunn. The former Governor had not been highly visible during the primary. His schedule had been light, with only a single event one or two days a week, usually with a safe Republican group. While engaging as a campaigner and polished as a speaker, Dunn seemed reluctant to gear himself up for the pace and physical commitment of a statewide race. As their candidate coasted through the uncontested primary, Dunn's campaign staff suffered from a misplaced overconfidence for which they later paid dearly. They correctly saw the urbane Dunn as a vastly superior media candidate to the overweight, bald beer distributor from West Tennessee. Some of Dunn's staff also appeared to have convinced themselves that nice offices, high salaries, Washington consultants and other trappings were evidence of a superior campaign organization.

In truth, the Dunn campaign was in disarray. Dunn had been forced to dump his original campaign manager, former Transportation Commissioner Bob Ferris, when it became clear Ferris had no clue about running a statewide campaign. Ferris had managed to spend nearly half the campaign's four million dollar budget in an uncontested primary. As Labor Day approached, the campaign had no plan and no meaningful strategy. The Republicans brought in their old trouble-shooter, former Finance Commissioner Lewis Donelson of Memphis, to establish some sense of order from the chaos. Donelson hired as his day to day operative Gary Cordell of Chattanooga, who was capable but had never managed a major campaign. Cordell's lack of experience was repeated in other key campaign slots, including press secretary, scheduler, research and event planning.

A mile away in McWherter headquarters, the opposite mood prevailed. In addition to a wealth of political experience among the senior staff, fifteen months of planning and execution had sharpened the skills and focus of the campaign. Schedules were precise and timely for both the candidate and the media. The candidate's stump speech had been written and refined. Events were advanced well, with proper attention to political protocol as well as small but important details such as parking, sound systems and food. Every aspect of Dunn's political and personal life was indexed and prepared for immediate response by the candidate or press office if needed. Organizations in each county had been established to put up yard signs, turn out crowds for events and handle election-day activities. The only significant problem had been a dissatisfaction with David Sawyer, the New York media consultant who seemed more intent on bilking McWherter's money than developing good ads. The campaign fired Sawyer and hired Bob Squier and Carter Eskew of Washington. The results were immediate. The new ads were sharp, stylish and clearly superior.

As Labor Day approached, the condescension of the Dunn campaign was well known among the McWherter staff. McWherter was behind in the polls, but within striking distance. In contrast to some of their counterparts, the McWherter camp looked forward to the fall with an enthusiasm that was genuine.

McWherter's strategy after Labor Day was straightforward. He would run a statewide strategy that conceded only the Second Congressional District. He would lose Knoxville, seek to break even in Memphis and Chattanooga, and win Nashville. He would break even or lose slightly in the Third and Seventh districts and carry the Fourth, Sixth, and Ninth districts by sizable margins. The key district was the First, where McWherter believed Dunn had a legacy of distrust and where McWherter had invested a larger than normal amount of time and money. If Dunn carried the First District with a traditional Republican majority, McWherter might need a huge majority in his home Eighth District to prevail. And if, as his staff believed, Mcwherter could become the first Democrat in modern times to carry the First District, Dunn's defeat could be crushing.

McWherter's campaign message was intentionally simple. The five-point plan was designed to respond to rural communities who correctly sensed they were being left behind by Tennessee's economic growth. At each stop, McWherter began with remarks about his commitment to "fix" the state's prison system and relieve the pressure on local jails to house state inmates. He then repeated his priorities of good schools, good roads, primary health care, clean environment and economic growth in all 95 counties. The speech evolved into what McWherter called a "95 County Jobs Plan." Its political purpose underscored McWherter's understanding that growth had to occur in rural counties as well as suburban Nashville. The fact that the plan had no details and no concrete strategy did not make it less appealing to rural voters who feared that without such a plan their communities would, in McWherter's favorite phrase, "dry up and blow away."

The Dunn campaign had trouble expressing a clear message. In early television ads and in speeches, Dunn sought support from business by emphasizing his opposition to repealing Tennessee's right-to-work laws. His comments were tailored to leave the impression that McWherter, as evidenced by his endorsement from organized labor, had a secret plan to repeal the right-to-work statutes once in office. McWherter brushed off the issue by declaring his commitment "to leave the right-to-work laws exactly as they are." Dunn's effort was an instance of trying to create an issue where none existed. Despite a lack of response from the media and business community, Dunn pursued the issue for weeks with little effect.

Dunn also had difficulty developing a message for education. As Governor, Dunn's most notable education accomplishment was the creation and funding of a statewide kindergarten program. Such an achievement could have been molded into the centerpiece of an appealing education platform packaged as the continuation of the education initiatives begun under Governor Alexander. Dunn could have spent five days a week during the primary visiting kindergarten classes and reinforcing his education credentials. Instead, his education message consisted of little more than a paragraph in each speech reminding voters he had started the kindergarten program 14 years ago. Dunn's education message appeared dated and a bit out of touch, and contributed to a similar feeling about his entire candidacy.

Dunn's inability to express a compelling message stemmed in part from his campaign's mistaken sense that the candidate was running for reelection instead of competing 12 years later in a new era against a stronger opponent. Recalling Dunn's successful initiatives from 1972 did little in 1986 to explain how he would respond to the needs of a state and an economy in transition. Indeed, his constant emphasis of past programs perhaps served to work against

Dunn, making him appear to be the candidate of the past while McWherter talked about "the revolution of change taking place in Tennessee." Voters were less interested in Dunn's creation of Tennessee's Department of Economic Development than his plans to attract jobs to depressed regions of the state. Voters who lived near polluted lakes and rivers cared little that Dunn had presided over Tennessee's first clean water laws. The Dunn campaign might have succeeded in developing a more clear and appealing message for the campaign's final thirty days. Instead, at the very time it should have reached full momentum, the campaign was thrown back on its heels and forced to defend the candidate against a variety of unexpected charges.

The McWherter campaign adopted early a strategy to neutralize voters' negative association with McWherter and alcohol. When Dunn criticized McWherter for selling beer, the campaign struck back quickly with documents indicating Dunn was a partner in ownership of Nashville's Vanderbilt Plaza Hotel, and as such held a liquor license for the hotel's bar and restaurant. While the media pressed Dunn to explain the difference in owning a beer distributorship and "owning" a bar, the McWherter campaign got a break when Bruce Dobie of the *Nashville Banner* reported Dunn had intervened on behalf of a friend's effort to get a liquor license in Greene County. Dunn seemed unable to explain the details of either issue. He pressed on with attempts to draw media attention to McWherter and beer. McWherter responded that Dunn's campaign treasurer Jim Haslam, owner of hundreds of Pilot convenience stores, was "the largest beer retailer in East Tennessee." The debate had shifted from an issue about propriety to one about hypocrisy that Dunn was clearly losing. Haslam called the McWherter campaign to urge a truce. With this call, the Dunn campaign voluntarily took off the table the one issue on which McWherter was most vulnerable.

The truce over alcohol did not mean that the McWherter campaign would let Dunn off the defensive. Since his tenure as Governor, Dunn had pursued a number of financial investments, many involving commercial and residential real estate. The McWherter campaign had devoted dozens of hours pouring over Dunn's financial statements and tax disclosures. The campaign reached two conclusions. Dunn had lost a considerable amount of money, much related to a failed condominium complex in Alabama. Not only had Dunn lost money, his tax statements left the impression that some of his transactions had not been fully reported to the Internal Revenue Service. The McWherter campaign argued internally whether to accuse Dunn of impropriety. Rather, the campaign opted to call on Dunn to explain his finances, a safer strategy and almost as effective.

Once again, Dunn appeared unfamiliar with the issue. His first response dismissed the issue as a private affair, followed by a feeble and unsuccessful attempt to explain a very complicated set of numbers and transactions. The most significant aspect of the crisis for Dunn was not whether he had participated in actions that were illegal or improper; he had not. When the story first broke, it was quickly evident that no one in the Dunn campaign had available any research about their candidate's financial activities. For several days, Dunn endured a painful and embarrassing series of media questions as his staff frantically attempted to gather and organize boxes of financial data. Every day on the defensive was a day lost to the campaign. The Dunn campaign finally held a press conference at which they displayed a variety of documents designed to prove Dunn's lack of wrongdoing. By this time, the McWherter campaign no longer cared. Their strategy to generate confusion and doubt had achieved its purpose. Dunn had only about 15 days left to make his case to the voters, and McWherter was loading his final bullet into the chamber.

No one in either campaign doubted that at some point McWherter would make an issue of the fact that since his term as Governor, Dunn had filed two IRS returns indicating he had paid no taxes. No amount of documents or television ads can explain convincingly to a majority of Tennesseans why persons with large incomes can avoid taxes. Wishing to concentrate its impact close to the election, McWherter waited until the campaign's last two weeks before beginning a coordinated effort to raise the issue. As he did earlier with Dunn's financial statement, McWherter called on Dunn to explain why for two consecutive yeas he "did not pay one cent in taxes." McWherter drove the issue home with hard-hitting television and radio ads, stressing that in the two years in question McWherter had paid several hundred thousand dollars in taxes. Dunn's ads responded unsuccessfully with claims that the ex-governor had paid "thousands of dollars" in taxes over a ten-year period. In the campaign's crucial last days, the Dunn campaign again found itself on the defensive instead of selling a positive message.

Several Republican leaders, particularly Governor Alexander, sensed the Dunn campaign was in serious trouble. Going into the crucial last days, the campaign was out of money. Furthermore, the relationship between Dunn and Alexander was strained. The former Governor and his campaign staff resented advice from the younger Alexander and his staff drawn largely from a media background. A weekend strategy session called by Alexander at the Executive Residence 17 days before the election produced a bitter exchange between Dunn and Alexander over Dunn's interpretation of polling data. Dunn took encouragement from a one point lead along with 22 percent of the black vote, a result he believed of his minority vote campaign called the "Quiet Storm." Alexander replied, correctly, that Dunn would never hold 22 percent of the black vote, meaning that Dunn in fact was trailing by several points with trends heading in the wrong direction. The discussion reportedly deteriorated with much blame and finger-pointing. To those who had watched Alexander for years, his campaigning for Dunn in the last days seemed uninspired.

Without frequent reality checks, campaigns have a way of making those closest to them believe the rhetoric of their press releases and lose touch with public sentiment.

The Dunn campaign entered the last week genuinely believing their candidate was three to five points ahead. So presumptuous were they of victory that the campaign placed an order for 64 telephones to be installed in the transition office for the following week.

McWherter, meanwhile, took advantage of the momentum during the campaign's final 30 days. The campaign was now scheduling eight to ten events each day, drawing crowds of several dozen in the afternoon and several hundred at evening rallies. As the McWherter campaign sought to tell the message in as many communities as possible, it made the serious mistake of over-scheduling the candidate. McWherter became physically exhausted, running the risk of saying something inappropriate to the press or collapsing on stage during a public event. He came close to both during a rally at the Ramada Inn in Nashville, causing his staff to cancel the campaign schedule for the weekend.

Until that point, the McWherter campaign had executed its strategy according to plan. Every Democratic faction, including the Ford family in Memphis, had been brought on board. Eskind and Fulton had appeared at public events, and Eskind's son Billy had been brought into the McWherter campaign. The state's congressional Democrats, as well as a large number of sheriffs and other local officials, were lined up to help get out the vote. Organized labor, the Tennessee Education Association and the State Employees Association also were solidly behind McWherter and ready to deliver. McWherter had worked hard to organize the black vote in Memphis, Nashville and Chattanooga. During this effort, his most valued endorsement came from the Student Government Association at Tennessee State University. Meanwhile, campaign political director J. W. Luna had effectively organized most of the state's 91 non-urban counties. Television and radio buys and newspaper ads for the campaign's last weeks were scheduled and in the can.

One other endorsement played a significant role in McWherter's campaign surge. Though a Republican, First District Congressman Jimmy Quillen had been a McWherter friend and a Dunn enemy since Dunn's veto of the medical school legislation. Quillen had ostensibly "buried the hatchet" with Dunn in a widely publicized ceremony, but those close to the congressman continued to believe Quillen fully intended to bury the hatchet in Dunn's back. Quillen's true intentions surfaced about three weeks before the election when he was responsible for an airport crowd hosting Dunn, Alexander and Vice President George Bush. The airport crowd was so embarrassingly small that the party moved quickly onto the plane without pausing for the customary remarks. The next day's papers noted that across the road from the airport at a middle school, McWherter's mother Lucille hosted a reception attended by more than 300 supporters.

Although the subject of much hype, the three debates with Dunn were largely uneventful. Dunn looked and talked like a Governor. McWherter put his opponent on the defensive during the second debate in Johnson City, the site of the medical school Dunn had vetoed 13 years earlier.

The debate was almost canceled when the McWherter campaign learned that Dunn, contrary to agreed upon rules, planned to fill the audience with campaign staff. McWherter threatened to withdraw and Dunn relented. In the third debate, Dunn found himself forced to explain his taxes and unable to mount an offensive. The debates probably had no clear winner or, from the perspective of the McWherter camp, no clear loser.

McWherter completed the campaign's final week with evening rallies in Knoxville, Chattanooga, Memphis, and Nashville, finishing in his hometown of Dresden. Dunn attended a rally hosted by singer Amy Grant in Brentwood while the McWherter campaign held a similar rally in Nashville with Jimmy Buffett. Dunn and McWherter both spent the last day on the obligatory statewide flyaround. Dunn was forced to borrow money for his last week's media buy. Although it drove his staff crazy, McWherter chose not to spend the remaining $400,000 of his campaign account on media, stating that the "money would only be wasted."

Election day saw steady rain in Middle and West Tennessee. Early returns gave McWherter a small lead that grew as the night went on. The election results were remarkably close to the campaign's strategy. As expected, McWherter lost the second district around Knoxville convincingly. He ran essentially even in the third and seventh districts. With a large rural turnout, he carried his home eighth district by a large margin, and won with strong majorities in the fourth and sixth districts. He carried the ninth district, running stronger than expected in Shelby County, and scored well in the fifth district around Nashville. In the key first district, the GOP base where Republicans often won with two-thirds majorities, McWherter tallied a stunning 53 percent of the vote. In Johnson County, one of the nation's most Republican counties and the site of his famous haircut, McWherter came with 47 votes of Dunn.

By nine o'clock, McWherter had built an eight point lead that was holding and grew to more than 100,000 votes. A television reporter at Dunn headquarters filmed a Dunn staffer crying uncontrollably while the campaign press secretary tried to put the best face on a race that was becoming a rout. Dunn called and graciously conceded to McWherter. For all his mistakes, Dunn remained to the end a gentleman. McWherter once again drove to the Hyatt Hotel, where the crowd was large and in a mood to party.

Several attempts were made after the election to explain McWherter's victory. One of the most simple, yet perhaps most accurate was offered by Jim O'Hara of the *Tennessean*. O'Hara pointed to a fundamental distinction in the message of the two candidates. When Tennesseans listened to Dunn, they heard a candidate who said, "I ought to be Governor." When they listened to McWherter, they heard a candidate who said, "I want to be Governor."

Many theories existed for McWherter's victory. Dunn gave away a tremendous opportunity by not campaigning more aggressively during his unopposed primary. The primary was a time when Dunn could have sharpened his message and planned his response to McWherter's anticipated attacks. The absence of a rigorous primary schedule left the Dunn campaign unprepared for the challenges and unexpected turns of the general election. By the end of the primary, the Dunn campaign had spent half of its limited resources with little to show for it.

Eliminating these mistakes still might not have been enough for Dunn to overcome McWherter. Republicans underestimated how hungry Democrats were for victory after eight years in the political wilderness. They also underestimated how hard McWherter was prepared to work for the prize. Some say the election was won in the summer of 1985, when McWherter plodded through one community after another gathering political and financial support. Others pointed to Republican complacency, while still others believed the key was a well-organized campaign that was able to keep his opponent on the defensive. Whatever the reason, McWherter's victory disputed a growing conventional wisdom that only candidates who project well on television can be elected in the age of electronic campaigns. By electing a bald, overweight, slow-talking beer distributor, Tennesseans demonstrated that issues count, and that planning, hard work and organization can still make the difference in statewide politics.

THE GOVERNOR

1987-1995

PART FOUR

THE GOVERNOR

1987-1995

One of democracy's greatest flaws is exposed when a newly elected governor is forced, quite literally, to create a government in the span of about 60 days. No corporate board would consider for a moment attempting to remove and replace the entire management structure of a multi-billion dollar company in so short a period of time. For a new governor, the physical and emotional demands of an extended campaign leave little opportunity for a candidate to devote more than occasional thought to the critical task of identifying the 40–50 individuals who will occupy key positions in a new administration. The challenge is further complicated by the immediate need to plan the Inauguration, a highly symbolic mixture of pomp, protocol and fundraisers that reveals much about the tone and management style of the new administration. The euphoria of winning the election, followed by the exhaustion that sets in the morning after, and the sudden shifting of gears from campaigning to governing make the transition period one of general chaos for even the most experienced politician.

McWherter was no exception. Beginning in 1984, his campaign on the whole had been methodically planned and executed over a two-year period. Suddenly, the replacement of a Republican administration that had been in power for eight years had to be organized and implemented in less than nine weeks. As is the case with most new governors, McWherter's values and priorities, as well as the management style that would come to characterize his administration, were reflected in the personalities and talent he assembled during the transition.

State government in 1987 had 21 executive departments and approximately 40,000 employees. Prior to the election, McWherter had a clear sense of the individuals he wanted for three of the most important Cabinet posts. All were extremely bright and highly regarded in their respective fields. Equally important, McWherter had known all of them for years in either a business or personal capacity. A key theme in McWherter's campaign was the notion that his experience as House Speaker would make him a "first day" governor. Building on this theme, McWherter quickly announced that his Finance Commissioner would be David Manning, a protégé of State Treasurer Harlan Mathews and a key financial advisor to McWherter during his tenure as Speaker and throughout the campaign. For Education Commissioner he selected Charles Smith, a Fulbright Scholar and the Chancellor of UT-Martin, located in McWherter's home county. His third announcement was Jimmy Evans of Dyersburg, a road builder with engineering and law degrees from Vanderbilt, to head up the mammoth Department of Transportation.

McWherter had privately intended for months to tap these three individuals. In terms of intellect, experience and loyalty, all were superb choices that reflected the same kind of careful planning that produced a winning campaign. After the announcement of these three selections, however, the process of filling out the Cabinet became swept up in the political forces that confront every new governor. Cabinets must have geographic balance. Women and blacks must be represented. In McWherter's case, he was obligated to primary opponents Dick Fulton and Jane Eskind, whose support in the general election had been critical to victory. Strong campaign assistance from the Farm Bureau and organized labor meant that these two key groups would have a strong voice in choosing the commissioners for Agriculture and Labor. McWherter's often-repeated commitment to state employees that he would not engage in a wholesale change of top management positions added pressure to retain one or more current commissioners. Finally, McWherter understandably wanted to reward a number of talented individuals who had worked closely with him in the legislature and in his successful campaign.

McWherter complicated an already difficult challenge with his next two announcements. As Commissioner of Conservation, he chose Elbert Gill of Memphis, the chairman of the House Committee on Environment and Conservation and a long-time friend. He also announced as the new Commissioner of Veterans Affairs Bill Manning, the Trustee of Gibson County and a war hero who had lost both arms and a leg in Vietnam. With these two selections, McWherter's first five appointments were white males, four of whom were from West Tennessee. The result meant that a very complex and diverse political garment had to be stitched together from among only 16 remaining Cabinet positions.

To organize the task, McWherter asked Jim Hall of Chattanooga to move from his role as campaign manager to director of the governor-elect's transition team. Well-liked by the campaign staff, Hall had the rare blend of political sensitivity and management skills required to bring order to an organization that is created, staffed and concludes most major business in a period that basically covers the Christmas holiday season. From the old State Office Building across the street from the Capitol, Hall dealt with the dozens of elected officials, large contributors, Democratic activists, campaign volunteers and other various hangers-on who aspired to jobs for themselves or their friends and families in the new administration.

Out on West End Avenue, a parallel process was taking place in McWherter's condominium, away from the crowds and distractions of the official transition headquarters. McWherter had chosen, but not yet announced, his two top aides. His Deputy Governor would be Harlan Mathews, the current State Treasurer and former Commissioner of

Finance who probably knew as much about Tennessee state government as any living individual. The new Chief of Staff was Jim Kennedy, McWherter's chief assistant since 1976. Every governor needs at least one senior advisor in whom he has complete trust. Both Mathews and Kennedy filled that need, although in different ways. Mathews was the senior statesman familiar with virtually every issue and personality in state government. A generation younger, Kennedy was more like a family member than a peer, with total commitment to executing McWherter's political agenda. Together, they played a key role in shaping the new administration.

McWherter, Mathews and Kennedy interviewed and ultimately selected the remainder of the administration's Cabinet and sub-Cabinet positions. They were joined on occasion by J. W. Luna of Manchester, the campaign's talented political director who later was named Commissioner of Personnel, and who later in the Administration was Commissioner of Environment and Conservation. Also present at some meetings was Carl Johnson of Sparta, a successful businessman who, although relatively new to the McWherter circle, had demonstrated adept fundraising skills during the campaign. Johnson would be picked to head up the Governor's Economic Development program and, later in the Administration, was Commissioner of Transportation. The fact that Luna and Johnson each led two large agencies reflected McWherter's confidence in their skills.

As McWherter sought names from across the state to fill out the Cabinet and sub-Cabinet positions in the various executive branch agencies, he looked inward to his longtime legislative aides to join Mathews and Kennedy on his personal staff. To manage the Governor's administrative affairs he brought in Betty Haynes of Columbia, who had served a similar role in the House Speaker's Office. Capable and professional, Haynes was often the quiet hand behind the curtain who endured the frequent playfulness of the younger staff while keeping a hundred details from flying off in all directions. For his Legal Counsel, McWherter chose Chief Clerk of the House David Welles, a former assistant district attorney from McWherter's home town of Dresden who had an exceptional blend of legal skills and legislative experience. His Policy Advisor was Billy Stair of Kingsport, also a veteran of McWherter's legislative staff who held a similar job in the campaign and who had worked closely with House Majority Leader Jimmy Naifeh on McWherter's legislative agenda. To oversee the Governor's security, McWherter selected long-time aide Steve Browder of Adamsville, a state trooper who had traveled with McWherter literally thousands of miles over the past several years and who eventually served as a colonel in the Highway Patrol. His day-to-day security was handled by Wayne Featherston of Hendersonville, who made an odd sight standing a foot shorter than the Governor he protected. Not surprisingly, McWherter chose as his personal assistant Madelyn Pritchett, a friend and employee who had worked with him for more than two decades. What proved to be one of his most popular decisions among the staff was bringing Alma and Billy Ford to Nashville from Weakley County to manage the day-to-day details of the Governor's Residence. Each of these individuals knew McWherter's priorities and expectations. Perhaps equally important, they all knew each other. The genuine familiarity among the Governor-elect and his Capitol staff was an unusual characteristic of a new administration and one that would help explain McWherter's success in the years ahead.

McWherter looked to his campaign staff to round out his Capitol team. Jim Hall became the Governor's Executive Assistant. Ken Renner, a former Knoxville Journal reporter who had ably handled media activities for the campaign, was named Press Secretary. Responsibility for legislative affairs was handed to Betty Anderson, a highly-regarded lobbyist for the Tennessee Education Association. The housing portfolio was assigned to Ken Jordon, who later became the first black general in the Tennessee Air National Guard. The ambiguous title of Special Projects director was given to Katy Varney, whose talent and creativity in the campaign had convinced McWherter that, whatever her title, her skills would be of value in the Capitol.

After a hectic series of recommendations, interviews and false starts, the Cabinet team came into place in the days before the Inauguration. In a gesture to the Fulton campaign, Mayor Fulton's wife Sandra was named Tourism Commissioner, joining Fulton's water and sewer director Bill Whitson as Commissioner of General Services. The Farm Bureau was pleased when long-time agricultural extension director A. C. Clark of Cookeville was named to head the

Department of Agriculture. Likewise, labor was comfortable with Labor Commissioner Jimmy White of Memphis, a leader in the Communication Workers Union. Rayburn Traughber of Chattanooga, the new Commissioner of Employment Security, Financial Institutions Commissioner Dennis Phillips of Kingsport, Revenue Commissioner Dudley Taylor of Knoxville, Commerce and Insurance Commissioner Elaine McReynolds of Nashville, Safety Commissioner Bob Lawson of Cleveland, and Mental Health Commissioner Eric Taylor of Memphis were brought into the administration with little or no previous association with McWherter. Two commissioners from the Alexander Administration, Jim Word in Health and Environment, and Steve Norris in Corrections, were retained. Finally, the massive Department of Human Services was given to a young woman who was perhaps the brightest and most talented of any appointee in the new administration, Nancy Ann Min of Rockwood. A Rhodes Scholar, a graduate of Harvard Law School and the first female president of the University of Tennessee Student Government, Min was the youngest Cabinet member in Tennessee history.

Despite the chaotic process in which many of McWherter's Cabinet and staff were selected, in the years ahead only two or three proved to be a disappointment. Indeed, McWherter would later suggest that the true secret to the success of his administration was not just an exceptional collection of talent, but a core group that stayed throughout the majority of his eight years as governor. In sharp contrast to the pattern of frequent turnover among the staffs of other governors, a remarkable number of McWherter's senior staff stayed six years, until the election in 1992 of Senator Al Gore as Vice President set in motion a series of moves to the new Clinton Administration that included Mathews and Hall. Manning, Kennedy, Stair, Haynes, Luna, Renner, Browder, Johnson, and Whitson stayed on until the last months of McWherter's second term. Few governors in Tennessee history enjoyed this level of stability—and loyalty—among their staff. Although the benefits were not always evident to outsiders, there were a hundred instances over the next eight years when the stability of McWherter's staff produced the experience and poise that made a critical difference between success and failure.

As if he did not have enough challenges, McWherter was confronted in early December with an unexpected controversy that threatened lasting damage to his relationships with the Legislature. A majority of the Senate Democratic Caucus, in a move that surprised many, voted to replace eight-term Speaker John Wilder of Somerville with Riley Darnell of Clarksville as the Democrats' nominee for Speaker in the upcoming session. Because historically the caucus voted as a block to support the nominee, and because Democrats held a 23–10 advantage in the Senate, Darnell's election appeared certain. Breaking tradition, however, Wilder sought the support of six Democrats to join with the ten Republicans to form a majority coalition and retain him as Speaker. As word of Wilder's plan leaked, anti-Wilder Democrats appealed passionately to the Governor-elect to intercede on their behalf, offering any number of deals to select a Speaker other than Wilder. McWherter was left in a no-win position. He could oppose the Senate Speaker with whom he had worked successfully for fourteen years, or he could decline to help Senate Democrats whom he had hoped would form the core of his legislative support for the next four years. In a decision motivated as much as anything by his personal belief in the separation of powers, McWherter chose to let the Senate crisis work itself out without his interference. Wilder's coalition prevailed, leaving extraordinary bitterness within a Senate now divided essentially into three camps— the ten Republicans, the seven Wilder Democrats, and the sixteen remaining anti-Wilder Democrats, or "Contras" as some jokingly likened them to the anti-government rebels in Nicaragua. Unfortunately, there was little joking in the Senate, where the atmosphere often was openly hostile. For more than two years, many of the senators barely spoke to one another. Some senators privately directed their anger at McWherter, whom they blamed for Wilder's election. The new Governor and his legislative staff were forced to factor this tension into every significant legislative issue in the Senate.

Meanwhile, the Inauguration came and went with relatively little fanfare. The day was bitter cold, but the crowd gathered on the War Memorial Plaza was large and enthusiastic. McWherter's remarks repeated the "95 County" theme that had played so effectively in the campaign, emphasizing that his administration would be one "in which no region would be favored, and none would be forgotten." After taking the oath of office, the new Governor played to the crowd by fulfilling a corny pledge he had made a thousand times in every campaign speech, claiming that after "a cup of coffee and four vanilla wafers he would be ready to be a first-day governor." (The pledge originally was two wafers, but since no one believed McWherter would eat only two, to be credible the campaign was forced to change the number to four.) To the cheers of the crowd, McWherter ate the wafers and drank the coffee, then moved off to the inaugural parade, where he watched 95 consecutive bands play "Rocky Top" as they marched in front of the reviewing stand. The Inaugural Ball at the Opryland Hotel featured Jerry Lee Lewis and a raucous, overflow crowd of Democrats. For at least one evening, the looming challenges of managing state government seemed far away.

On Monday morning, the new Governor began the real task of running a government. For McWherter, "being governor" brought a unique challenge. He had served as House Speaker longer than anyone in Tennessee history, and his political instincts were naturally shaped by his experience and the peculiar traditions of the legislative process. While outsiders might view being House Speaker and Governor as similar leadership positions, they in fact are very different roles that require different talents and different approaches to governing. The Legislature by definition is a reactive body, with the responsibility to take recommendations from the

Governor and adopt, reject, or modify them. The role of the executive branch is to recommend laws or policies that can improve existing programs or, in some instances, create completely new programs to meet an important public need. McWherter's task in the early months of his administration was to make a transition from Speaker to Governor that was much more complicated, and that required a much greater change of leadership philosophy and personal style, than many observers imagined.

Much of McWherter's considerable success as Speaker, and later as a candidate for Governor, was based on political instincts learned as a young aide for Congressman Fats Everett of Union City. Among these instincts was a belief that the public felt government enacted too many new laws and should back away from trying to manage people's lives. He was probably correct, but he also knew that the public looks to the Governor to lead the way in addressing major issues such as education and health care. As Speaker, McWherter was comfortable in letting the process bring issues and proposals to him and his legislative colleagues for disposition. In his early months as Governor, he was predictably less comfortable introducing the traditional administrative legislative package that usually contained a handful of truly important bills and two or three dozen minor bills recommended by the various executive agencies. Introducing a large number of bills, whether warranted or not, simply was counter to the political instincts he had developed over the past 18 years in the legislature.

1986 campaign "send-off." Wanting to stage his official announcement for Governor in East Tennessee, the campaign held an old-fashioned send-off rally the evening before on the courthouse square in Dresden. Seated on the stage are Congressman Ed Jones, McWherter's mother Lucille and son Mike.

The son of a sharecropper, McWherter was enormously popular in Tennessee's rural communities. A huge rural vote in 1986 provided his margin of victory. *Tennessee Library & Archives*

Repubican allies. Support from Congressman Jimmy Quillen of Kingsport and Representative Ralph Cole of Elizabethton was a key factor in McWherter's 1986 campaign for governor. *Tennessee Library & Archives*

1986 Inauguration. From left, Mike McWherter, Lucille McWherter, Harlan Mathews (in hat), Congressman John Tanner, Governor McWherter, and Jimmy Naifeh (in trench coat).

Deputy Governor Harlan Mathews, with wife Pat, after appointment by McWherter to the U.S. Senate. State Treasurer and Finance Commissioner under previous administrations, Mathews was a peer to McWherter and a mentor to many of McWherter's younger staff. *Tennessee Library & Archives*

Senior Policy Advisor Billy Stair, Finance Commissioner David Manning and Chief of Staff Jim Kennedy listen closely to a press conference. All three worked for McWherter as House Speaker and stayed the entire eight years of his Administration, providing stability and continuity. *Tennessee Library & Archives*

Conferring with Senator Al Gore, Jr., at the Executive Residence. During Gore's 1988 presidential bid, McWherter helped secure endorsements from every southern Democratic governor and speaker except Bill Clinton. *Tennessee Library & Archives*

Conducting an interview with Jim Hall, Billy Stair and Nancy Ann Minn at the 1988 Democratic Convention. After Bill Clinton's election as President in 1992, Hall became Chairman of the National Transportation Safety Board and Min joined the White House policy team.

J.W. Luna, left, was a close political advisor who served in two Cabinet positions. Russ White served as Commissioner of Health during the transition from Medicaid to TennCare. *Tennessee Library & Archives.*

David Welles, left, worked for Mcwherter as Chief Clerk of the House and later as Counsel to the Governor. Carl Johnson served as Commissioner of Economic Development and Commissioner of Transportation. *Tennessee Library and Archives.*

House Speaker Jimmy Naifeh whispers to Deputy Governor Harlan Mathews at weekly 7:00 a.m. breakfast with House and Senate leadership. The meetings promoted bi-partisan cooperation by keeping open lines of communication. *Tennessee Library & archives.*

Canoeing the Pigeon River heavily polluted by Champion paper mill in North Carolina. McWherter was nearly arrested by the North Carolina sheriff, who claimed the Governor was "trespassing on Champion's river." His decision to deny the mill a water quality permit produced tension on both sides of the state line at Cocke County.

Bill-signing ceremony for education reforms. The delegation of five Democrats and five Republicans indicates the bi-partisan nature of the sweeping reforms that included a new funding formula and higher standards for teachers and students. McWherter viewed the reforms as the highlight of his political career. *Tennessee Library & Archives*

With President Bill Clinton. McWherter was a frequent sounding board for
Clinton, as Governor of Arkansas and later as President. In November 1993
Clinton's help was critical in gaining a federal waiver for TennCare. *Tennessee
Library & Archives*

McWherter's Cabinet, 1991. McWherter credited a highly-talented Cabinet
for much of his success. Remarkably, while some changed roles, twelve Cabinet
members remained throughout his entire term as Governor. *Tennesseee Library &
Archives.*

Laughter before the storm. In typical fashion, McWherter breaks into laughter with members of the General Assembly moments before he announces his plan for tax reform. Although his tax reform plan was rejected, the Legislature approved and funded his 21st Century Schools program. *Tennessee Library & Archives*

In January 1987 the situation was made worse by a severe shortage of time needed to prepare for a legislative session. In most years bills are drafted and budgets prepared in the fall months. The majority of McWherter's time in November and December had been devoted to organizing his administration. The limited hours not spent on discussing and interviewing potential Cabinet members were dedicated to preparing the new state budget. These competing priorities, when combined with McWherter's bias against introducing new bills, meant that the Governor's first legislative package was an unusually small one.

The Governor's legislative agenda did contain one major initiative. A series of abuses in nursing homes had generated substantial statewide media coverage and made nursing home "reform" a campaign issue. McWherter had promised to seek civil penalties for what he believed to be the relatively small number of nursing home owners guilty of serious infractions. He faced serious and well-financed opposition by the nursing home industry, which for a period stone-walled against civil penalties of any kind. The challenge was an important one for several reasons. By taking on a powerful lobby in his first legislative session, McWherter sent a message that, in contrast to what some had predicted, he would not "play it safe" by refusing to give the Legislature hard choices. As the owner of a nursing home, the new governor made clear his willingness to forgo personal interests. By achieving passage of the reforms, he quickly reinforced the notion that his political skills as Speaker would be transferred to the 1st floor of the Capitol. Finally, the nursing home legislation was viewed by most as a "liberal" initiative on behalf of the old and helpless. McWherter's victory in passing a comprehensive nursing home reform package turned on its head a frequent complaint that he was an old-fashioned conservative incapable of creative ideas.

The other dominant issue in the 1987 legislative session was less pleasant. Virtually all new governors are frustrated by the lack of budgetary flexibility they inherit from their predecessors. Invariably, they feel the bureaucracy is overstaffed with political appointees and that many programs are unnecessary or mismanaged. Some of this criticism comes from an arrogance that is a common byproduct of campaign rhetoric and tends to exaggerate both the scale of problems and the ability of the candidate to solve them. In many cases, however, the frustration is based in fact. Any administration that has power for eight years will accumulate employees and programs of marginal value that are a drain on limited state revenues. The situation in 1987 was no different.

The boldest move of McWherter's first 90 days in office, and the one that in many respects defined his first administration, was a decision to make major cuts in his first proposed state budget. Despite a one-cent sales tax increase in 1984, recurring commitments by the Alexander Administration, particularly in the areas of K-12 and higher education, by 1987 had consumed almost all of the projected growth in the state's sales tax revenue base. McWherter's first budget confronted him with a serious dilemma that threatened to derail his Administration before the train got out of the station.

In the wake of a resounding campaign victory, McWherter suffered from unrealistic expectations on the part of Democrats who had been out of power longer than any period in modern Tennessee history. From constituencies such as teachers, sheriffs and state employees to county party chairs seeking patronage jobs for their friends, these groups were anxious for McWherter to deliver quickly on what they believed to be commitments to jobs and additional funding made in the campaign. Most of these groups did not understand or care about the details of the state budget or the fact that McWherter had little money available to satisfy these requests. Instead, they believed that it was simply "their turn" and that a new Democratic governor should have little trouble doing what they genuinely believed all other governors had done in the past.

McWherter indeed probably could have avoided at least a portion of the short-term problem by hiring several dozen employees at county transportation garages and human service offices. He also might have been able to satisfy a small number of budgetary requests. In doing so, however, he would have made certain that going forward his Administration would have no ability to develop any meaningful programs in education, corrections, economic development or any other area without raising taxes. Reflecting his fundamental fiscal conservatism, McWherter chose to cut the state budget sharply, with substantial layoffs of state employees and little or no raises for teachers. The decision generated considerable frustration and grumbling among Democratic legislators and constituents statewide, some of whom openly criticized the new Governor. Despite some carping, the Legislature adopted the budget. The initial public reaction was mostly unpopular, but the long-term impact was decidedly more positive. By significantly lowering the base of the budget's recurring expenditures, McWherter was able to provide the opportunity in future budgets for the level of revenue growth needed to implement his campaign agenda.

McWherter's first legislative session contained one other initiative that had more far-reaching consequences than many realized at the time. The Governor requested, and the Legislature granted, broad authority to negotiate incentive packages with companies considering investments in Tennessee. Called the TIIPS program, the authority allowed McWherter to bid against other states with commitments for water and sewer, job training and tax abatements that did not require legislative approval. Funded each year by the Legislature, the TIIPS program required a great deal of confidence in the Governor's honesty as well as his negotiating skills. Passage of the proposal was a reflection of McWherter's personal relationship with a majority of legislators. As measured by the number of large investments over the next eight years, the program proved to be as valuable as any enacted during McWherter's Administration.

McWherter's ability to succeed or, in the view of some, to survive, in his first legislative session was due in large measure to the help he received from a number of senior legislators, many of whom had served with him during his tenure as Speaker in the House of Representatives. McWherter's coalition remained in tact in the House, where for four years he received the strong support of Speaker Ed Murray and later his successor Jimmy Naifeh, whose skills as Majority Leader resulted in the passage of every Administration bill during McWherter's first term.   The initial House leadership team that consisted of former McWherter colleagues Murray, Naifeh, Lois DeBerry, John Bragg and Matt Kisber—and that later added Majority Leader Bill Purcell--was talented, cohesive and of enormous value to the new Administration. McWherter also received consistent help in the Senate, although tensions among the three Senate factions made the effort more complicated. As hostile as the personal relationships were among some senators, the hostility did not on most occasions boil over into partisan fights that threatened to block the Administration's legislative agenda. Indeed, each of the three Senate factions had members who had served with McWherter in the House, including Democrats Tommy Burks, Ward Crutchfield, Riley Darnell, Milton Hamilton, Bill Owen and Majority Leader Carl Moore. McWherter also enjoyed good rapport in the Republican Caucus with Minority Leader Ben Atchley, Leonard Dunavant, Randy McNally and Curtis Person—all former House colleagues. McWherter's personal relationships with these House and Senate leaders on more than one occasion enabled the

Administration to overcome what otherwise might have been legislative train wrecks.

As he moved through his first legislative session, McWherter also benefited more than many realized from the advice and political support of three of the state's constitutional officers. Elected by the General Assembly, the Treasurer, Comptroller and Secretary of State historically have not always been close to governors who sometimes view them as adversaries. In McWherter's case, Treasurer Steve Adams, Comptroller Bill Snodgrass and Secretary of State Gentry Crowell were not only long time friends, but also extremely knowledgeable of Tennessee's budget and tax structure. Using their expertise as unofficial financial advisors to the Legislature, throughout McWherter's tenure the constitutional officers played an important role in bringing the Administration and the General Assembly together on major financial issues.

After the adjournment of the 1987 legislative session, McWherter turned immediately to the most pressing challenge facing his Administration. Despite historic increases in the state's prison population during the late 1970s and early 1980s, as of 1985 the Alexander Administration— while they opened new prisons funded under Blanton--had not proposed or funded any new prison facilities.

The inevitable result was a prison system characterized by overcrowding, idleness and violence. The situation exploded in October 1985, when inmates rioted and burned two buildings at Turney prison. With the corrections system on the verge of collapse, the federal courts took over Tennessee's prisons. The state agreed to a consent order that placed the prisons under the oversight of a federal Master appointed by the court. The consent order provided the Master, Patrick McManus of Minnesota, with extraordinary authority to make decisions about issues such as population caps, double-celling of inmates and the size and cost of new prisons. The appointment of McManus as federal Master created the atmosphere for an inevitable collision between McWherter and the court. McManus believed that Tennessee, instead of quickly enlarging its prison system to accommodate the influx of new prisoners, should actually reduce the inmate population from about 10,000 to 7,000.

In effect, McWherter inherited a consent order that threatened further chaos in the prison system and a public outcry if thousands of criminals were released for lack of beds. To make matters worse, as of May 1987 an endless series of oversight committees and meetings had produced virtually no progress on two new maximum security prisons funded in the November 1985 special legislative session. Meanwhile, the judicial system was like a bent hose with the spicket turned on. Thousands of convicted prisoners who could not be transferred to the state prisons were backing up in county jails, creating additional political pressure from sheriffs and local officials who looked to McWherter with increasing frustration for a solution. When a federal court in Chattanooga subpoenaed Correction Commissioner Jeff Reynolds and Policy Advisor Billy Stair to explain why the state could not take convicted prisoners from the Hamilton County jail, the Governor faced the dilemma of having one federal judge telling him to release inmates and another telling him to take more.

"Grabbing hold" of the prison system represented perhaps the ultimate test of McWherter's management skills. In some respects he viewed restoring management discipline in Tennessee's prisons as a personal challenge more interesting than other, more policy-oriented issues such as education or health care. His approach reflected his personal style. He visited every prison, something no previous governor had done. He became directly involved with every aspect of the corrections budget, from staffing to food costs. He assigned Stair to work full-time with the correction system. Working closely with the Legislature's Corrections Oversight Committee, the short-term goal was to get the two new prisons designed and built faster and cheaper. The longer term goal involved building a safe and humane prison system that was large enough to handle the explosion of convicted felons without bankrupting the state. McWherter's personal involvement energized the process. Knowing the Governor was watching, decisions got made and stayed made. Gradually, the corrections system regained confidence and got back on its feet.

After the first chaotic five months, McWherter devoted the majority of his time in 1987 to completing the organization of the Administration and his first love, recruiting economic investment. His calendar was filled largely by private meetings with companies contemplating investments or by public groundbreakings and openings of new factories such as the Denso plant in Maryville and Brothers Industries in Bartlett. In between, McWherter's new position required entertaining a large number of celebrities, ranging from Princess Anne of Great Britain to weatherman Willard Scott of NBC's Today Show. Some of the celebrities he enjoyed more than others.

By 1988, the new Administration had settled into a rhythm. The budget cuts of the previous year had their intended impact. With a lower budget base, revenue growth was sufficient to give McWherter the chance to address some of his more modest campaign goals. Among the most visible was a pledge to increase the beginning salaries of teachers to $18,500. Even what appeared to some as an extremely low salary bar was out of reach to dozens of counties with a deteriorating tax base. By raising the salary floor, McWherter also indirectly increased salaries for a large portion of Tennessee's 35,000 teachers.

The 1988 session witnessed other education initiatives of a minor scale. The Administration undertook to recruit more minority teachers. Low key efforts were underway to tackle a Career Ladder program that was tangled in an expensive evaluation process that was losing credibility. Finally, the Department of Education, long a dumping ground for former school superintendents, was reorganized and streamlined. None of these education initiatives alone was viewed by the Legislature or the public as particularly bold or innovative. Only four years after the divisive turmoil of the 1984 legislative fight over performance-based pay, the education system was not ready to absorb radical change. Taken together, however, McWherter's small initiatives helped gain the confidence and support from teachers that he would later need when time came for more ambitious education reforms.

The spring of 1988 brought a series of economic good news stories that bolstered the Administration. Bridgestone announced that the company's corporate headquarters would move to Nashville from southern California. Groundbreaking ceremonies took place for Kellogg in Memphis and Nippondenso in Maryville. Part of the success was due to long-term efforts that preceded McWherter. Equally true was the fact that several companies came to Tennessee because of McWherter's personal involvement and his ability to offer incentives that did not require legislative approval.

For McWherter, much of the spring and early summer of 1988 was focused on the presidential bid of Tennessee Senator Al Gore, Jr. Gore had surprised many by entering the primaries against the favorite, Massachusetts Governor Michael Dukakis. McWherter quietly worked a number of his colleagues, both governors and speakers, in the southern states. He was successful in securing the endorsement of Gore from every southern Democratic governor but one, Governor Bill Clinton of Arkansas. As Clinton hedged, most of McWherter's staff assumed he was positioning himself to secure the Vice Presidential nomination if Dukakis defeated Gore.

On Super Tuesday, Gore swept through the southern primaries and took the delegate lead for the Democratic nomination. Despite this momentum, Gore had yet to prove he could win outside the South. After a series of losses, he gambled heavily on winning in Wisconsin, and lost. His campaign was over before the California primary.

Anyone who attended the Democratic Convention in Atlanta knew that Dukakis was doomed. Selling him to the country was tough enough. Selling him to Tennessee voters was impossible. The high point of the convention for McWherter came when a reporter from ABC asked if McWherter was worried about the ACLU. McWherter got a serious look and said, "Yes, yes I am. We play them in two weeks and I don't think we can beat them." It was about the only time anyone laughed during the Dukakis campaign.

Apart from the presidential election, in 1988 the most visible issue in Tennessee, or at least in East Tennessee, was the controversy over the pollution of the Pigeon River by the Champion Paper Mill in Canton, North Carolina. Located about ten miles upstream from the Tennessee state line in Cocke County, the paper mill for 80 years had discharged industrial waste that turned the small river into the color of Coca-Cola. Not only had the paper mill eliminated fishing and recreation on the river, many residents in the Tennessee communities of Newport and Hartford believed the river had contributed to higher than normal levels of cancer.

By the late 1980s opposition in Tennessee to the paper mill had reached an emotional state, with newspapers and public officials calling on McWherter as Governor to refuse the renewal of a water quality variance needed by the paper mill to continue operation. In the fall of 1988 angry citizens wearing black armbands packed the auditorium of Cocke County High School for a public hearing on the river conducted by the State Department of Health & Environment.

In Canton, Champion threatened to close the mill and lay off 2,000 workers if McWherter denied the variance. Within the Governor's staff, some feared that if the issue was decided in court the state might be "out-lawyered" by Champion's high-powered legal team. As tensions rose on both sides of the state line, the possibility for violence became real.

McWherter's approach to the Pigeon River said volumes about his style and thought process. Without publicity, he traveled early one September morning with Billy Stair and an agent of the Tennessee Wildlife Resources Agency to Canton. The group loaded a canoe into the river just up stream from the paper mill, where the water was pristine. They floated past the mill directly through the black discharge that bubbled up around the canoe. A few hundred yards past the mill, they pulled the canoe over to the river bank, where they were met by the local sheriff. McWherter instructed Stair to "handle it" while he stayed with the canoe. In an unpleasant tone, the sheriff informed the group they were trespassing. When Stair suggested that the river instead belonged to the public, the sheriff replied with a single comment that captured more than eighty years of arrogance by Champion toward the people of Tennessee: "Y'all are trespassing on Champion's River."

The sheriff in North Carolina did not arrest the Governor of Tennessee, but from that moment the only doubt left about McWherter's decision on the variance was the timing. He chose to deliver the decision as a Christmas present to the people of East Tennessee. He gave Deputy Governor Harlan Mathews the thankless job of calling Governor Jim Martin of North Carolina on Christmas Eve to deliver the news. The celebration that followed in Tennessee carried McWherter out of 1988 on the highest note yet of his first two years in office.

McWherter always had, at least in general terms, a clear sense of his direction. His primary goal as Governor was to bring Tennessee's rural communities into the state's economic mainstream. In speech after speech since 1985, he said that counties needed four key components to have a chance to compete. The first three categories were predictable—good schools, good roads, and affordable and accessible health care. The fourth category was a surprise to some. McWherter correctly insisted that having a chance for economic growth also required that counties possess the ability to manage their solid and hazardous wastes.

By 1989 the Governor had developed a strategy to implement most of the 95 County Jobs Plan. McWherter had personally redesigned much of the Department of Transportation's long range road construction program to emphasize connecting rural areas to the interstate system. His staff was compiling the data and quietly working with neighboring states on a strategy to provide regional solid waste programs for rural counties and an interstate compact to handle Tennessee's toxic wastes. Education Commissioner Charles Smith was working with the State School Board on a new school funding formula that would determine both a school system's needs and its relative ability to fund those needs. The solution to the health care piece was less certain, but remained a frequent topic of internal conversation among the Governor and his staff.

Meanwhile, the Governor had also developed a strategy to remove gradually the state's prison system from federal control. New maximum security prisons, expanded and redesigned to reduce staffing requirements, were opened in Davidson County and under construction in Lauderdale County. Legislation to establish a Boot Camp for young offenders was enacted and a facility built in Wayne County. The juvenile corrections system was reorganized into the new Department of Youth Services with new facilities in Jefferson and Davidson counties. Equally important, the state had successfully challenged the federal master on the issues of double-celling and the placement of a population cap on the system. Although still a long way from being out the woods, the Correction Department was clearly moving in the right direction with a new found confidence.

The economic good news continued. McWherter participated in new plant announcements in Kingsport, Morrison, Lewisburg, Greeneville and Smyrna. The most celebrated event was the opening of the Saturn plant in Spring Hill. With Saturn, Tennessee's emerging role as a major player in the automotive industry was established. McWherter participated in the Saturn grand opening, riding in the first car off of the assembly line. As the television cameras recorded the historic moments, the public relations experts had failed to realize that a Saturn was not designed for persons who weigh 270 pounds.

What turned out to be the most important event of 1989 did not occur in Tennessee, but in Charlottesville, Virginia, where in September President George Bush hosted the nation's governors for an Education Summit. In the University of Virginia Rotunda, designed by Thomas Jefferson, Bush implored the governors to take aggressive steps to raise standards and funding for education. While joking with fellow Governor Bill Clinton, McWherter seemed genuinely to take to heart the President's message. Although the details of an education reform plan had not yet taken shape in his mind, the Governor brought back to Tennessee a personal commitment to make substantial and lasting reforms in the state's education system.

As 1990 dawned, McWherter wrestled with a personal decision that was among the most difficult of his career. After 14 years as Speaker and three years as Governor, he had accomplished most, if not quite all, of his personal goals. He had become comfortable in the role of Governor. He had reorganized and professionalized much of state government, particularly in the departments of Transportation and Correction. He had placed the state on a firm financial foundation. Business investment was taking place at a record pace, with many of the new jobs steered into the state's rural counties.

Most Tennesseans assumed that McWherter would seek a second term in which he would take on the larger and more challenging issues of education reform and, some hoped, reform of the state's antiquated tax system. Only those closest to McWherter knew that he was seriously considering not running for a second term. They understood what few outsiders could believe, that McWherter was not driven to elected office in the way that many others are. He viewed being Governor as a genuinely hard job that takes a physical and emotional toll. He was not intoxicated by the power of the office. He felt, rightly, that there should be no moral obligation to run for a second term, and that good government can be served by elected officials who do their best for a short time and then simply go home. Above all, McWherter could not stomach the idea of going through another grueling campaign like the one in 1985–86. On many days he felt that he had done a good job and was ready to quit the political grind and go back to his farm in Dresden.

From a private perspective, McWherter's children had married and begun families. His daughter Linda had received her doctorate from Ole Miss and married Steve Ramsey of Carroll County. They had two boys, Brett and Matthew. Meanwhile, McWherter's son Mike had graduated from Vanderbilt Law School and clerked for Supreme Court Justice William Fones. He later joined the law firm of Donelson, Stokes and Bartholomew, one of Middle Tennessee's largest and most successful firms, and married Mary Jane Wooten of Covington. The couple also had two children, Walker Ray and Mary Bess. Having lived largely alone for more than a decade, McWherter during this period often preferred visiting with his growing family to the endless demands of the Governor's Office.

McWherter's decision to run for a second term was motivated by two factors. Perhaps most important, the Republican Party struggled to find a credible candidate to oppose the popular Governor. The Republicans floated a succession of names, followed in each case by denials of interest as each assessed his chances. Former Finance Commissioner Bill Sansom of Knoxville and State Representative Brad Martin of Memphis took their names out of contention. So did Watergate Defense Counsel and actor Fred Thompson of Nashville. The party's top fundraiser, Jim Haslam of Knoxville had signaled his lack of enthusiasm to raise money for a Republican candidate. Ron McMahon, publisher of the pro-Republican *Knoxville Journal,* made clear his support for McWherter. Without the commitment of the party's senior leadership and without traditional editorial support, the Republican nomination was of little value. The only person who would pick up the Republican standard against McWherter was one-term state representative Dwight Henry of Cookeville.

As the likelihood of serious Republican opposition diminished, McWherter increasingly focused on the possibility that a second term might provide the opportunity to undertake historic reforms of the state's education and tax systems. In early 1990, while he did not know clearly what his proposed changes would be, his core philosophy guided him on both issues. He understood the obvious, that the old education funding formula that provided state funds in each school system on the basis of headcount was broken to the point that dozens of communities could not operate their schools. Likewise, he believed that a tax system based on the sales tax was grossly unfair to the working poor. McWherter was, if nothing else, a fiscal conservative, but his positions on these two issues illustrated his progressive belief that government exists to provide a more level playing field for those who work hard but who are penalized by a system with forces beyond their control. Based largely on the hope that he could take on these two issues in a second term, McWherter announced his re-election bid at Rocky Mount, the site of his original announcement for Governor in 1986.

Playing it safe, McWherter had few initiatives in the 1990 legislative session. His most significant proposal was the Hazard Waste Planning Act, in which Tennessee, Kentucky, Alabama and South Carolina agreed to a complex plan to incinerate, recycle and bury the hazard wastes generated in each of the four states. The legislation, which survived a last-minute effort by North Carolina Governor Martin to eliminate Tennessee, was quite progressive for its time and gave Tennessee a substantial advantage in the effort to recruit industries that generated large amounts of waste by-products. The Administration's other notable legislative effort was an early signal that McWherter could be both serious and creative about new ways to address education problems. In an effort to curb Tennessee's high drop out rate, the Legislature enacted a statute that revoked the drivers license of persons under age 18 who dropped out of school. In two years, Tennessee's drop out rate declined 27 percent.

The remainder of the spring was spent largely on positive events. McWherter appointed the state's first female justice, Martha Craig Daughtrey, to the Supreme Court. A second maximum security prison was opened at Fort Pillow. In Middle Tennessee, McWherter announced proposals to construct Interstate 840 around Nashville. The Governor presided over a Drug-Free Tennessee conference attended by hundreds of students and organized by Jim Hall. As schools adjourned for the year, the Department of Education released SAT test scores that were the highest in two decades. The fact that most Tennessee students did not take the SAT was not emphasized in the announcement.

While running a campaign for reelection, McWherter also used the majority of 1990 to lay the groundwork for major education reforms. He employed a two-part strategy designed to shore up his political base across the state while simultaneously building public support for fundamental changes in the governance and funding of Tennessee's education system. His plan was a blend of something old and something new. He gathered his cabinet and sent them on the road to each of Tennessee's 139 school systems. In each community, they visited schools, met with teachers and students, and held a public meeting. The meeting was highlighted by a high-quality video that made a compelling case for increased funding and modern technology for Tennessee's schools. Entitled "21ˢᵗ Century Schools," the video for its time was a sophisticated new way of communicating policy initiatives to the public.

In the course of more than 200 school visits, McWherter repeatedly heard two messages from parents and community leaders. In one school after another, parents complained that they had no meaningful way of knowing how well—or poorly—their teachers and students were doing. Grades in one community had no relationship to grades in another. Even test scores, long used as a measure of performance, were based upon school systems as a whole, and did little to tell parents about the quality of individual schools or individual teachers. Against the backdrop of this lack of accountability, many parents also felt they had no real voice in the management of their local schools. With many school systems politically divided by bickering between elected school boards and elected superintendents, the attempt to understand what local schools needed and how to make the system respond was a source of constant frustration.

In dozens of rural systems, this frustration combined with a growing inability to fund basic services such as textbooks and school buses, leading many citizens to believe the time had come for fundamental changes in Tennessee's K-12 education system.

As ideas for his education reform package began to take shape, litigation before the state Supreme Court provided McWherter the perfect pretext for an overhaul of Tennessee's school finance formula. Ruling on a case brought by 77 rural school districts, the court in 1990 declared that the state's system of funding K-12 schools on a headcount basis was unconstitutional by virtue of discrimination against districts in which the local sales tax base was insufficient to provide the minimum level of textbooks, science equipment and other core materials needed for a basic education. In effect, the court gave the Governor and the General Assembly one year to restore "equity" to state funding, with the clear implication that if the Legislature failed to act the court would redistribute funds from wealthier districts to poor ones. The court's ruling sent a shock wave through the state's urban and middle-sized systems, which stood to lose millions in funding. With the state's prisons already under court control, the specter of the state courts taking over Tennessee's schools quickly led to a consensus that virtually any alternative was preferable.

For McWherter, the court's threat could not have come at a better time, leaving the Governor and his staff feeling as if they had been thrown into the briar patch. In late

1990, the state School Board completed a year-long study that recommended the components of a "Basic Education Program," or BEP, that represented the fundamental "tool box" needed for each school to provide an adequate education. Working out of the spotlight in the State Office Building across the street from the Capitol, Finance Commissioner David Manning was fine-tuning a new school finance formula that funded the new BEP based upon a county's ability to fund its schools, as measured by sales taxes, property taxes, and personal income in each county. Meanwhile, Education Commissioner Charles Smith and Senior Policy Advisor Billy Stair were putting the final touches on a broad range of other education reforms that would include governance, curriculum, performance standards, and parental involvement. While legislators anticipated that McWherter would introduce an education package to the 1991 session General Assembly, most would later be stunned by the scope of the proposals. Unfortunately for McWherter, his education package was not the only proposal that stunned the Legislature.

What should have been a festive second inauguration was turned into a somber occasion by the impending war in Iraq. After Iraq's invasion of Kuwait in the summer of 1990, President George Bush had ordered the preparation of an American effort to retake Kuwait and protect the oil fields of Saudi Arabia. Thousands of Tennessee National Guard troops had been called up in the weeks before the January inauguration. McWherter made it a point to attend every deployment ceremony. At each he invited any member of the troops to meet with him privately if they had an issue of personal concern. Several did. The majority were worried about the inability to pay their mortgages while overseas. McWherter appealed to the state's banks, asking them to suspend the mortgage payments of Tennessee soldiers for the duration of the conflict. Most of the banks readily complied, even though they had no legal obligation to do so.

With war imminent, McWherter thought it inappropriate to have the bands and balls usually associated with an inauguration. The inauguration was limited to the official ceremony on the War Memorial Plaza. In his speech, McWherter pledged to "commit the remainder of my public service to the goal of providing a 21st Century classroom for the young people of Tennessee." He added, in words that were analyzed carefully, "I will do all within my power to ensure that, if we raise revenues, we do so in a way that is fair to the working men and women we represent." The meaning was clear to those who understood the code. McWherter planned to pay for his education package with a tax on income.

In an attempt to keep the focus, at least for a time, on his education package, McWherter separated the announcements of his education and tax proposals. He unveiled his education reforms on January 31, 1991, in the State of the State message before a joint session of the General Assembly. Pledging "to dedicate the rest of my public service to rebuilding our community schools," McWherter asked the

Legislature "to help me bring about fundamental changes in the management, the standards, and the accountability" of Tennessee's education system.

The scope of the proposed changes was sweeping. McWherter recommended that all school boards be elected and empowered to appoint and terminate superintendents. In turn, superintendents would hire and evaluate principals. The proposed appointment of superintendents would affect the status quo in more than 60 school systems and represented one of the most controversial of the proposed reforms. As a balance to this imposed change in local governance, the state Department of Education abolished some 3,700 rules and regulations over issues as mundane as the number of water fountains and the size of playgrounds required at local schools.

The legislation also proposed major changes in the areas of curriculum and graduation standards historically reserved for the State Board of Education. McWherter urged that the number of core courses required for graduation be increased from 11 to 13 and include more history and civics. The 8th grade-level proficiency test for graduation would be removed and replaced with more rigorous subject-area tests. In a controversial move, the General Track diploma, with no focus on either college or vocational preparation, would be abolished and replaced with a more focused two-track path.

Equally controversial was a radical proposal for measuring performance and accountability. With the bipartisan support of Republican Senator Ray Albright of

Chattanooga, chair of the Committee on Education, and his colleague Democrat Andy Womack of Murfreesboro, McWherter recommended adoption of a "value-added" testing procedure designed to measure the annual progress of systems, schools and individual teachers. The Department of Education would publish the testing results each year in the local media for the benefit of parents and the community. School systems that scored well would receive incentive funding up to five percent. Continued poor performance could result in the removal of the superintendent and the school board. Again, in an effort to address the anxieties of teachers about the new evaluation, McWherter recommended that the average class size in grades K-8 be reduced from 25 to 20 students.

Finally, and most significant, McWherter sought to overhaul the school funding formula by providing state funds based upon the relative wealth of a local community. The State School Board would establish the minimum education "tools," or Basic Education Program, needed to provide an education in each school system. Counties such as Davidson and Knox, with large tax bases, would receive less than two-thirds of their BEP funding from the state, while poor counties such as Hancock might be funded nearly 90 percent by the state. The key to the proposal was that no county would experience a reduction in funds. Unspoken, but understood, was that a tax increase would raise all the boats, some more than others.

Despite philosophical concerns about elected superintendents and confusion about the new funding formula, reaction to McWherter's proposed education reforms was generally positive. The good feeling lasted exactly 28 days. In a joint convention on February 28, McWherter followed his proposal to reform education with a second proposal to reform Tennessee's antiquated tax system. Taking the legislators methodically through his reasons why a sales tax, property tax and lottery were neither fair nor adequate, the Governor concluded, "If we choose to do what is fair, and to do what is best for the future of Tennessee, then tax reform is the road we must travel."

His remarks proposed the most far-reaching financial changes in Tennessee history. The entire sales tax on food would be removed, as would the state sales tax on residential water. The state sales tax rate on all other items would be lowered from five and a half percent to four percent. The state franchise tax would be lowered 20 percent. These reductions would be offset by a four percent flat tax on adjusted gross income, a rate that McWherter proposed to cap in a constitutional referendum. The tax reform package was estimated to raise an additional $290 million, all of which McWherter insisted be earmarked to fund his education proposals.

While the education package enjoyed broad support, the tax reform legislation never got off the ground. The new Democrat leadership in the House—Speaker Jimmy Naifeh and Majority Leader Bill Purcell—lined up behind the proposals. But in the Senate the Democratic leadership, including the Speaker and the Majority Leader, refused to sponsor or endorse the Governor's tax bill. With the leadership's public rebuke of McWherter, chances of getting majority support in the Senate were nonexistent. For the first time, the generally good feeling of the previous four years among legislators and the Administration was replaced by tension and open criticism. McWherter was forced to find a Republican Senate sponsor for the tax bill, which quickly died before any meaningful attempt to gather support. Because McWherter had insisted that "the funding come first," the death of tax reform also meant the death of the education bill.

The spring and summer of 1991 brought the low point of McWherter's administration. The failure of his education and tax reforms was followed by deep cuts needed to balance the state budget. After months of anticipating funding increases, local schools were hit by a sharp decrease in state revenues for education. Many systems were in chaos, unable to operate their school buses or buy textbooks. Jails were overcrowded and state agencies with dozens of unfilled vacancies could not renew drivers licenses or process other basic services. The optimism of the previous year had been replaced by a growing concern that things were not going to get better.

Despite the Legislature's rejection of his tax reform proposal, McWherter continued to believe it was possible to gain approval for some version of a tax on income. He looked to Governor Lamar Alexander's experience in 1983, when the Legislature rejected his education package.

Alexander called the Legislature into Special Session in 1984 and achieved passage of his education plan and a one cent sales tax. Alexander also called a Special legislative session in November 1985 to deal with the prison crisis. McWherter hoped that a similar strategy, which focused the attention of the media and the Legislature on a single topic, would provide the boost needed to move his tax reform legislation. He also believed that the turmoil of the current school year, caused by state budget cuts, might be enough to motivate a majority of legislators to support his plan.

On January 14, 1992, McWherter addressed the General Assembly called into Special Session. He once again made the case for his education reforms, most of which the Legislature supported. His tax reform proposal, however, had been modified substantially. Gone was the removal of the sales tax on food, the most popular part of his original plan. The tax rate on adjusted gross incomes had been reduced from four to three percent, but the state sales tax rate had been reduced only one-half cent.

McWherter had altered his tax proposal in the hope that it would be more popular than his first plan. The result was just the opposite. In the words of the House Majority Leader, "Those against tax reform don't like it, and those in favor of tax reform don't like it." The leadership of both chambers made clear that the new tax reform bill had no chance. The Special Session adjourned in less than three weeks.

McWherter immediately filed his education package in the regular session, accompanied by a one-half cent increase in the state sales tax. Both bills were enacted within six weeks. The year-long argument over the income tax had served to take the spotlight off many details of the Governor's education plan. When finally enacted, the 93-section bill contained very few amendments and was remarkably similar to the original 1991 proposal. Most important, Tennessee put in place the most far-reaching change in education funding since the state began providing free textbooks in the 1940s. From 1992 to 1998, state funding for K-12 education increased more in Tennessee than any state in America. The impact on the state's rural counties was among the most lasting changes of McWherter's administration.

The success of McWherter's sweeping education reform package was to a large degree overshadowed by the failure of his effort to change Tennessee's regressive tax system. The failure predictably was the subject of much second-guessing. Some accused McWherter of never really trying to pass a tax on income. Others believed he could have succeeded with a different plan. Still others insisted he could have passed his original plan if the income tax had been subject to a statewide referendum. Conspiracy theorists suggested that the entire tax reform proposal was part of an elaborate strategy to manipulate the Legislature into defaulting to an increase in the sales tax.

While all of these notions may seem plausible, none recognizes what tax reform supporters found difficult to accept: that a vocal majority of Tennesseans simply did not trust the state legislature to implement a tax on income that would not be raised in the future. The fact that for four years McWherter had cut the size of state government, or that Tennesseans had one of the lowest per capita tax rates in the nation, did not matter. During the decade of the 1980s, the most articulate and persuasive political voice in the country was Ronald Reagan, who repeated at every opportunity the message that government "was not the answer, but the source of people's problems." One unintended consequence of Reagan's message was a dramatic drop in the public's confidence in all forms of government, from the White House to the courthouse. In community after community, local governments could not pass school bond referendums. In Nashville, a dramatic proposal to replace the sales tax on food with a tax on income, regardless of how fair the idea sounded, simply could not gain the public's trust.

McWherter recognized this skepticism. He also recognized that even if a bare-knuckled fight brought passage of the tax reform proposal, the victory would likely result in the loss of Democratic majorities in the Senate and House. Likewise, he understood clearly that a crushing defeat could erode most of his political capital for his second term. The fact that in the face of these risks he went forward with a tax reform initiative says much about the depth of his personal philosophy and his willingness to accept the political consequences.

This does not suggest that McWherter's tax reform strategy was not flawed. His first plan, on the whole, was viewed even by many opponents as more fair to working

Tennesseans and a more practical way to operate state government's finances with greater predictability. His second plan was neither, and was based largely on a short-sighted effort to gain votes. With both plans, McWherter's greatest miscalculation was in not anticipating how the Senate's internal turmoil would prevent the ability to form a coalition of support. Senators who had historically spoken in favor of tax reform now felt they could no longer trust some of their colleagues to deliver on a previous pledge to vote for an income tax. Passage of tax reform would have been a monumental effort under the best of circumstances. With the key element of trust removed, the task became impossible.

McWherter realized in the early days of the 1992 Special Session that his goal of reforming Tennessee's tax system was hopeless. Although disappointed on a personal level, the Governor almost immediately turned his attention to passage of his education reforms, funded with a half-cent increase in an already regressive sales tax. His quick transition gave rise to questions about his commitment to tax reform. These questions ignore the fact that his ability to go forward immediately without recrimination may have been the only way to salvage his education package.

The passage of McWherter's education reforms signaled a sharp turn in the fortunes of his administration. From that point on, good news followed in 1992. Prison and jail overcrowding finally was eased by the opening of new prisons in Clifton, Tiptonville and Nashville. The Department of Education released the state's first annual education report cards, giving parents and the media a real snapshot of how the local schools were performing. After a difficult year, the administration received some measure of consolation when Tennessee was named by *City & State* magazine as the nation's best managed state government.

The fall of 1992 was, at least in some respects, as dramatic as the spring. The presidential election campaign had rapidly evolved from a runaway for incumbent George Bush into a toss-up. When, after endless vacillation, New York Governor Mario Cuomo decided not to run, the surprise Democratic nominee was Arkansas Governor Bill Clinton. Few in the national media were aware that Clinton had burst upon the political scene in Tennessee in October 1991 at the annual Jackson Day Dinner at Nashville's Opryland Hotel. The scheduled keynote speaker was Senator Jay Rockefeller of West Virginia. During the banquet dinner, Rockefeller became seriously choked on a chicken bone and was rushed to Vanderbilt hospital in an ambulance. Faced with a crowd of 1,000 Democrats and no speaker, McWherter and Senator Jim Sasser huddled urgently while Rockefeller was being attended to by medics. "We just need somebody to give a five-minute talk and get out of here" was McWherter's suggestion. By pure coincidence, Clinton had been in Nashville that day on business with his wife Hillary. The Governor and Hillary paid a courtesy visit to McWherter for a drink at the Executive Residence and accepted a last-minute invitation to attend the Democratic event. With few options after Rockefeller was taken to the hospital, McWherter asked Clinton if he would tell a joke or two and make a short partisan speech. Clinton obliged. Witty, articulate and with just the right tone of righteous partisan indignation, he gradually captivated the audience, many of whom at first were more interested in getting the World Series score of the Atlanta Braves. By the end of Clinton's remarks the entire room was standing, cheering, and sharing the kind of laudatory comments that are rarely heard at the standard "rubber chicken" political dinners. No one who witnessed Clinton's coming out party that night doubted that the Arkansas governor left Nashville with the support of Tennessee's Democratic activists.

Clinton brought another surprise the following summer with the selection of Tennessee neighbor Al Gore as his vice-presidential running mate. Tennessee suddenly was front and center in the national campaign, with McWherter again actively involved on behalf of his southern friends. McWherter officially introduced the pair of baby-boomer candidates to the national media on the steps of the courthouse in Carthage. The Clinton-Gore message of change resonated well with an electorate that felt Bush had squandered his popularity with a do-nothing agenda. Helped by third-party candidate Ross Perot of Texas, Clinton and Gore won handily.

The victory presented both an opportunity and a challenge for McWherter, who needed to name a replacement for Gore in the Senate. His initial plan was to appoint Congressman John Tanner of Union City, a protégé and former state legislator when McWherter was speaker. When

Tanner unexpectedly declined, McWherter was left with no immediate back-up plan. Over the next several weeks he was besieged by persons who coveted the Senate appointment. His eventual choice to replace Gore was Deputy Governor and close friend Harlan Mathews, who had also served as State Treasurer and State Finance Commissioner over a period of nearly four decades. Mathews was joined by Executive Assistant Jim Hall, who left to become chairman of the National Transportation Safety Board, and Human Services Commissioner Nancy Ann Min, who became White House Special Assistant to President Clinton.

Their departure represented the first major realignment of McWherter's inner circle. Even before the departure of Mathews and Hall, the Governor benefited from a deep bench of talent that had been developing in the Capitol for much of his Administration. Rather than reach out to new and unfamiliar faces, McWherter for the most part looked to his bench to occupy key vacancies among his cabinet and staff. Kennedy and Stair together filled the vacuum left by Mathews. David Gregory, Estie Harris, Beth Winstead and Gina Coakley coordinated affairs with the General Assembly, comprising one of the best legislative teams seen on Capitol Hill. Jim Hall's work with Drug-Free Tennessee was handed to his longtime assistant Carol White. When Chief Counsel David Welles was appointed to the Criminal Court of Appeals, his Deputy Burney Durham assumed greater responsibilities in support of new Counsel Diane Neal. Rich Riebeling, a talented former staffer for

Nashville Mayor Dick Fulton, followed Johnny Hayes as Commissioner of Economic Development during a period of exceptional activity. Former legislator Cotton Ivey was named Commissioner of Agriculture.

McWherter's management philosophy led to a number of career state employees being given the chance to lead executive agencies and key support functions. Russ White was promoted to Commissioner of Health when the agency was reorganized, enabling J.W. Luna to lead the difficult challenge in Environment and Conservation. Similarly, when Jeff Reynolds left as Commissioner of Correction, he was replaced by Christine Bradley, a former warden and the nation's only female corrections commissioner. In similar fashion, Talmadge Gilley became Commissioner of Financial Institutions, Jim Davenport was promoted to lead the Employment Security, Don Holt became the new Commissioner of Personnel, Bob Grunow was promoted in Human Services, Wayne Qualls moved up in Education, and Betty Adams led the new Department of Children Services. Carl Johnson, the former Commissioner of Economic Develop, was brought back to head up Transportation.

In the Capitol, the departure of Deborah Seivers as the Governor's Scheduler was filled ably, first by Raymond Thomasson and later by Eunice Golden. Likewise, the promotion of McWherter's personal staff assistant Paul Willson was backfilled by Jimmy Evans. Each of these individuals was highly competent and required little "on-site" training.

The collective talent of this "second wave" of commissioners and senior staff proved more important than most observers realized at the time. After nearly two years of legislative struggles over education and tax reform, many around the Capitol anticipated that McWherter might ease back, take on few controversial issues, and basically cut ribbons for the remainder of his administration. Instead, 1993 proved to be the most active and most productive twelve months of McWherter's career. Some would argue that 1993, at least in a political sense, was among the most successful years in Tennessee history.

With two years remaining as Governor, McWherter had in place three of the four buildings blocks for his 95 County Jobs Plan. The road program was fully funded and redesigned to connect rural areas to the interstate system. Many of the same counties for the first time had a regional plan to manage solid and hazardous wastes. The sweeping new education reforms were moving hundreds of millions of dollars in additional state funds to rural school systems. The only remaining piece for the jobs plan was a need to provide affordable health care to about 500,000 working Tennesseans with no health insurance. In what many regarded as the best speech of his career, McWherter's 1993 State of the State message framed not only his accomplishments, but also the final challenge that he believed would provide the foundation for long term economic growth.

Unknown to all but a handful of McWherter's staff, Finance Commissioner David Manning and his assistant

Manny Martins were quietly working on a radical proposal that would place Tennessee's $3.2 billion Medicaid system under managed care. With a plan first scribbled on the back of an airplane napkin, Manning and Martins were convinced that market forces could save hundreds of millions of dollars in the public sector by introducing the same competition that had slowed health care costs in the private sector. They were supported by a task force study led by Phil Bredesen and Vanderbilt heart surgeon Bill Frist that concluded the Medicaid system was hopelessly broken and that only a complete financial restructuring of health care could avoid bankrupting the state. (In time, Frist would become U.S. Senate Majority Leader and Bredesen would become Mayor of Nashville and later Governor.)

On April 11, McWherter addressed a joint session of the General Assembly, warning legislators that "in the absence of a revolutionary change in Tennessee's health care system, by the year 2000 health care will consume more than half the revenues of state government." He blasted what he called the "Hocus Pocus" strategy of generating ever more state provider fees from hospitals "in order to feed our addiction to federal matching funds." The Governor asked rhetorically why Tennessee should support a Medicaid program that reimbursed $500 to hospitals for a vaginal delivery in Bristol and $5,000 for the same procedure in Nashville. Denouncing as irresponsible a program that without question paid "any fee, for any service, at any time," he proposed what he termed "the most radical health care plan in America." Named TennCare, the new plan promised to save $6.5 billion over five years by placing the Medicaid population as well as the working uninsured in a managed care program that would offer services to the lowest bidder.

Faced with the choice of cutting $764 million from the state budget or placing their hopes on McWherter's plan, a majority of legislators took the leap of faith. Passage of the TennCare legislation did not, however, mean the new program would go into effect. The federal Department of Health and Human Services vehemently resisted Tennessee's proposed withdrawal from the Medicaid system and placed every possible bureaucratic obstacle in the way. The strategy was to drag on the negotiations until it became impossible to implement the TennCare program in January 1994. Exasperated, McWherter flew to Washington to ask personally for President Clinton's help. During his meeting with McWherter, Clinton phoned DHS Secretary Donna Shelala and directed her—in language that was unambiguous--to remove her agency's objections to TennCare. McWherter received notice of tentative approval from Shalala on November 18. Formal approval came on December 22, only ten days before the new plan was scheduled to go into effect. After an extraordinary effort to notify doctors, hospitals, pharmacies and patients, TennCare became operational on January 1.

As was the case with many of McWherter's major initiatives, the new health care plan defied conventional ideological description. By transferring a multi-billion dollar government fee-for-service program to a managed care program in the private sector, TennCare could rightly be called one of the nation's most "conservative" approaches to health care reform. By extending coverage to more than one-half million working uninsured, TennCare was at the same time among the most liberal health care initiatives undertaken by any of the fifty states. The rare blend of populism and free-market conservatism found in TennCare was, to a greater degree than many realized, a classic reflection of McWherter's personal political philosophy.

In the short run, TennCare delivered the promised financial savings. For three to four years, TennCare's competition among managed care providers squeezed, depending upon one's viewpoint, several billion dollars out of the system and slowed the annual rate of growth in health care spending to a level at or near the rate of inflation. In time, TennCare's inability to restrain ever accelerating cost increases was brought on by a number of events that eventually led to the program's collapse. In part because of vigorous federal opposition, TennCare's implementation was rushed, leading to widespread confusion and a loss of credibility among insurance and health care providers that was difficult to regain. The rush to implement the program also resulted in the approval of managed care providers that, although successful as small companies with 10,000 or fewer clients, stumbled badly while attempting to make the transition literally overnight to 100,000 TennCare clients. Patients' records were lost while hospitals and doctors went unpaid.

Both businesses and insurance companies learned to game the system, cherry-picking lower-cost clients and dumping large numbers of high-risk employees and catastrophic care patients into TennCare, creating huge deficits for hospitals such as the UT Medical Center. Meanwhile, the state acceded to a series of consent orders in federal court that essentially forced the TennCare program into providing an ever-wider range of open-ended services. Although outright fraud in the program was never as widespread as critics claimed, virtually every Tennessean had heard an anecdote of fraud that further eroded public confidence in TennCare. Faced with these challenges, during the period from 1994 to 2002 when decisive leadership and stable management were most critical, the TennCare program went through eight managers in eight years. No major insurance company in America could have survived such management turmoil. TennCare was no exception.

Despite a premise of health care delivery that many still believed to be valid, TennCare ultimately could not be salvaged. Faced with financial collapse, the program was eliminated by Governor Phil Bredesen in 2005 and replaced by necessity with a program that was less ambitious and less constrained by the federal courts. At TennCare's inception McWherter knew, and often emphasized publicly, that the program would have to be modified as years went by. Despite TennCare's ultimate fate, McWherter had few regrets about his effort to extend health care coverage to Tennessee's working families.

In contrast to the intense battle over TennCare, the rest of 1993 was largely a series of successes and good news, much of which represented the culmination of hard work from the previous six years. In March the initial infusion of $37 million for technology provided the first computers that many schools systems had ever known. In May *City and State Magazine* ranked Tennessee, for the second year in a row, the nation's best managed state government. In June the state's Rainy Day Fund reached the record level of $150 million. In July McWherter kicked off the state's Bicentennial Celebration with the groundbreaking of a new mall below the Capitol. In August the Department of Education announced the high school drop-out rate had fallen by 27 percent. In November the Chronicle of Higher Education ranked Tennessee's universities the "most improved" in the nation.

One of the year's only disappointments came at the end of the most intense industrial recruitment effort of McWherter's Administration. For more than a year, Tennessee had joined more than two dozen states in a fierce competition for a major investment by Mercedes-Benz in the German automaker's first North American assembly plant. Tennessee had put together an attractive package of incentives, hoping to lure Mercedes to the site of the never-completed Clinch River Breeder Reactor near Oak Ridge. McWherter had been involved personally in the negotiations, visiting the Mercedes headquarters in Stuttgart and secretly hosting a German delegation on a house boat in Oak Ridge.

By most accounts, Tennessee had made the "final four" short list, in a close race with North Carolina and slightly ahead of Virginia and Alabama for the plant that would employ some 5,000 workers.

As the Germans neared a decision, they did what all large companies do prior to investments of this scale, playing the states against each other to achieve the best terms. To McWherter, the eleventh-hour negotiations made clear that Alabama had opened its checkbook and appeared willing to pay virtually any price to win. By coincidence, during an October trade mission of the southern governors at the New Otani Hotel in Osaka, Japan, Mercedes announced the company's decision to build their new assembly plant in Vance, Alabama. As later reported in the *Wall Street Journal*, the state of Alabama had indeed made an unprecedented offer, agreeing to pay the first year's wages of the new employees and even pledging to place the Mercedes symbol of German industry on top of Birmingham's Legion Field, a gesture that some thought ironic at the stadium named in honor of the soldiers that defeated the Third Reich.

How the various governors received the news said a great deal about their personal styles and philosophy. Governor Jim Hunt of North Carolina was genuinely surprised and visibly angry, with comments that probably would have been better left unsaid. Standing across the room from Hunt, McWherter congratulated Alabama Governor Jim Folsom, explaining the win simply by saying that "Alabama was hungry" and wishing Alabama and

Mercedes well. Later in his hotel room, the former shoe salesman explained his comments, observing that Mercedes' Alabama plant would need a large number of suppliers, many of which were already located not far up Interstate 65 in Tennessee. Mercedes indeed appreciated McWherter's gracious comments, and over time signed contracts with several tier-one suppliers in Tennessee.

December, in some respects, was the crowning month to a remarkable year. In addition to achieving approval for TennCare, Tennessee's rate of unemployment fell to the lowest in state history, from one point above the national average to a point and one-half below the average. More significantly to McWherter, the number of counties with double-digit unemployment had dropped from 40 to eight. On December 7, McWherter appointed Adolpho Birch as the first black member of the state Supreme Court. Finally, McWherter received the ultimate Christmas present. After a contentious eight-year struggle, the federal court returned control of Tennessee's prisons. During McWherter's tenure, Tennessee's corrections system had moved from having only one accredited prison facility to being the only state in which every prison was fully accredited. During the same period, the McWherter Administration had constructed more prison beds than all previous Tennessee governors combined. Local jails were relieved of overcrowding. In the state prisons, both new and old, violence was dramatically down. By abandoning labor-intensive guard towers and adopting new technologies and architectural designs, the per-inmate cost of operating the facilities was reduced by one-third.   In returning the prisons to the state, the federal magistrate characterized the state's progress as "remarkable."

McWherter's final State of the State message in 1994 summarized his Administration by echoing the comments in late December of a bond rating agency that had recently evaluated the state's finances. Sitting in McWherter's Capitol office, the group's leader had remarked, "Mr. Governor, we've been all over this country and I've got to tell you, there's something magical going on in Tennessee."

"When many states can't seem to get past goals and task forces, how can Tennessee pass and fund some of the most sweeping education reform plans in the country? When the prisons in two-thirds of the states are under federal court order, how can it be that Tennessee has the only fully accredited prison system in America? When there are states that continue to have enormous budget shortfalls, why does Tennessee have the largest rainy day fund in its history? When our neighbors have had to cut funds for higher education, how can it be that over the last two years Tennessee has increased funding for higher education more than any of the fifty states? How does one explain why health care reform is gridlocked by the special interests in state legislatures across the country, while in Tennessee we are embarking on the most creative new health care program in history?"

McWherter's answer to these rhetorical questions captured the essence of a political strategy that was as genuine as it was practical. "We have emerged among the nation's leaders in economic growth, in education reform, and in health care reform because no governor in America could have a legislature more responsible and more cooperative than the Tennessee General Assembly."

Engaging in nostalgia, McWherter recalled looking at other states that did not "resist the temptation to take the quick and easy solution," choosing to float bonds, dip into the pension fund or roll debt into future budgets. "I took a hard look at that road, and I decided as governor it was my responsibility to lead Tennessee down a less traveled path."

Three weeks later McWherter's final budget address provided financial context for many of these accomplishments. His 21st Century Schools program already had funded 2,100 new teachers to lower class size and equipped 4,200 classrooms with computer technology. His last budget provided K-12 schools with another $125 million in new funds, adding 1,400 more teachers and equipping 650 more classrooms. The budget funded another 1,000 prison beds, expanding the correction system more than all previous Tennessee governors combined. The proposed funding increase for TennCare was six percent, roughly one-third the rate of past Medicaid increases.

Delighting in one of the state's most prosperous periods in history, the legislature gave bipartisan support to all of McWherter's budget proposals and refrained from enacting changes to TennCare despite the tremendous turmoil among doctors, hospitals and patients that accompanied the program's implementation.

The final seven months of McWherter's administration were largely an exercise in celebration of continued good news. In June the Governor dedicated the Bicentennial Mall, stating his belief that "our time on this earth is more than just a brief moment of light between darkness." In July the state reported that 340,000 working uninsured Tennesseans had health care coverage under TennCare, giving Tennessee the largest percentage of residents in the nation with health insurance. In August Tennessee's economy was ranked the nation's fifth strongest. In October the University of Memphis, where as a freshman he had failed to make the football team, dedicated the new Ned McWherter Library. In November *Governing Magazine* named the native of Palmersville "Public Official of the Year" for the entire United States.

On December 29, McWherter received what may have been the final validation of his tenure as Governor. The state Department of Employment Security announced that Tennessee's unemployment rate had dropped to 3.6 percent, the lowest in history and lower than the national average for 40 consecutive months.

In the final days of his administration, McWherter expressed the pride he took in these accomplishments in a speech to the Nashville Kiwanis Club. "The Circle of Life has turned, and the sun has risen and set and risen again on Tennessee. The next governor and the next generation will inherit a future that those of us born before the Second World War could have only dreamed about."

Becoming philosophical, he summed up a journey that was shaped decades before in the farms and factories, and by the people who touched his life in West Tennessee. "For nearly eight years, I have done my best to be worthy of you, and very simply, to be one of you. Together, we have fought the fight. We have kept the faith. We have finished the course."

"After 26 years of public service, the shadows are falling on my career. But as these shadows lengthen, the sun is rising on a younger generation of Tennesseans who will know a day that never came when I was young. It will be a day when the world looks to find the very best, and it will be the day when their eyes turn to Tennessee."

ACKNOWLEDGMENTS

I am indebted to the many people without whom this story of Ned McWherter could not have been written. Katie High gave up more hours than I could count gathering a thousand details about McWherter's early life. She retrieved mountains of materials, organized them and drafted what became the basis for the first chapter of the story. The fact that Katie never worked for McWherter made her contribution all the more appreciated. We could not have finished this project without her.

Many of Katie's notes were provided by Richard Nanny of the University of Tennessee at Martin, whose interviews with McWherter produced some of the book's most revealing anecdotes. Doug understood better than many that the Ned McWherter Tennesseans knew in the latter part of the 20th Century was a man shaped by events and personalities that touched his life decades earlier.

I also owe special thanks to Gerald Reed of the Secretary of State's Office and his wonderful staff at the State Library of Archives who helped me locate and select historical photographs. Archivists Marylin Bell Hughes, Tom Kanan, Susan Gordon and Karina McDaniel went through hundreds of archival boxes, photo sheets and newspaper clippings. State Photographer Jed DeKalb's memory of "special" shots he took over the years was invaluable. Darla Brock of the Manuscripts Division provided more help and patience than I was entitled.

Vickie Conner did a tremendous job of designing the book's layout and maintaining her poise as I changed my mind. Her skills are superb.

Just like he did twenty years ago when I was a junior staffer, Harlan Mathews gave me sound advice about the book's tone and style. Now as then, I resisted at first, eventually realizing that as usual Harlan was right.

Finally, I need to thank my wife Carmella and my daughter Taylor, who had to endure night after night as I sat in front of the computer. For all you put up with, I thank you from the heart.

INDEX

McWherter, Linda, 21, 39, 88, 147

McWherter, Lucille Golden Smith, 1-2, 5, 7, 9, 13, 21-22,
    34, 39, 41, 88, 112

McWherter, Mike, 21, 35, 39, 87, 147

McWherter, Ned Ray

    Anheuser Busch, 33

    Bay-Bee Shoes, 16

    Childhood in Michigan, 5-7

    City Café, 7-8.

    Eagle Distributors, 35

    Elected to Legislature, 40

    Elementary School, 3

    Football, 17-18,

    Future Farmers of America, 11-12

    High School, 7, 11-16,

    Martin Shoe Company, 22-26, 32

    National Guard, 18-20,

    Nursing Home, 35-37

    Puerto Rico, 26-30

    Race relations, 5, 8-9

    Volunteer Distributing, 35,

    Volunteer Express, 38-39

    Campaign for Governor

    Advance Team, 88, 82

    Alcohol, 107-108

    Announcement, 92-93

WITHDRAWN